EDITIONS

Publishers of Architecture, Art, and Design
Publisher: Gordon Goff

www.oroeditions.com
info@oroeditions.com

Published by ORO Editions

Project Coordinator: Jake Anderson

10 9 8 7 6 5 4 3 2 1 First Editions

Library of Congress data available upon request.

ISBN: 978-1-935935-64-3
Color Separations and Printing:
ORO Group Ltd.
Printed in China.

International Distribution:
www.oroeditions.com/distribution

ORO Editions makes a continuous effort to minimize
the overall carbon footprint of its publications. As
part of this goal, ORO Editions, in association with
Global ReLeaf, arranges to plant trees to replace
those used in the manufacturing of the paper produced for its books. Global ReLeaf is an international
campaign run by American Forests, one of the world's
oldest nonprofit conservation organizations. Global
ReLeaf is American Forests' education and action
program that helps individuals, organizations, agencies,
and corporations improve the local and global environment by planting and caring for trees.

PWP LANDSCAPE ARCHITECTURE: BUILDING IDEAS

In memory of Daniel Urban Kiley, who through his lifetime of design challenged us, instructed us, mentored us, and was always a supportive friend.

TABLE OF CONTENTS

INTRODUCTION: BUILDING IDEAS AND OUR READINGS OF THEM

John Dixon Hunt

Things morph, like firms, ideas, landscapes—and of course the
culture that shaped them (or should have done). And yet . . . .
Some ideas that continue to sustain landscape design are central
and, therefore, *mutatis mutandis*, permanent. I would, conservatively,
name just three: that landscape design must be seen and seen to
be an art not "nature"; that the past is ever present; that reception
is as important as design.

There is no point in designing a landscape—be it rural, urban,
commercial, community-based—that does not proclaim itself as a
design. This may take the form, traditionally, of knowing that we enter into that space from another, a liminal experience whereby we
recognize that we have moved from one landscape into another
that is distinguished by things that are here but not there. It can be
the planting or furniture that strikes us; it can be an unusual layout
of paths or features that are endemic to the making of outdoor
spaces, like viewsheds. These things are borrowed from the world

outside design—what the Late Renaissance called the two natures of wilderness (landscape of the gods) and cultural sites (ports, roads, fields)—but they are now reified, epitomized, abstracted into what is thought to be a third nature. Peter Walker has been an exceptional mover into that third nature.

Landscape design is also an art, whether or not the designer sees himself or herself as an artist. Yet it is also an art that (unlike others) may succumb sooner rather than later to changing fashions because—simply—it is an art that is used in a way that sculpture and painting and music and literature are not.

The philosophy of beauty is not taught these days in schools of landscape architecture, and, indeed, that aesthetic debate is complicated and requires a good philosophical mind to guide us through its quicksands and labyrinths: not least— see below—because these days we rarely share any consensus on beauty. It was a problem that started early enough when rivals of "Capability" Brown who thought his work was no better than "common fields" invoked a different set of criteria for assessing landscape design. But it is constantly at issue in modern and especially minimalist painting.

Dan Kiley urged Pete Walker to go to see Villandry and Sceaux, as well as other Le Nôtrean sites; but nobody would ever think that Kiley was just imitating those extraordinary places in his own work. Nor does Walker. It is incidentally crucial that Kiley sent Walker to those sites that we awkwardly call "formal" or geometric because if he had urged the sites of "Capability" Brown, it would have been less instructive since it might have deterred Walker (at least for a while) from espousing a wonderfully visible play with a formal repertoire.

One of the endemic frustrations of trying to teach the history of landscape architecture is that some students resent and so turn their backs wholly upon the past. Yet writers read books that have been written before and do not therefore try to write the same thing: Alexander Pope "imitated" Horace, but those poems are ineluctably Pope's. I suspect that once they are out of graduate school, it is far easier for at least a few talented designers to accept and realize that current designs involve a thoughtful and critical recognition of the hinterland of design—its forms, yes,

Marlborough Roof Garden

Peter Walker, Martha Schwartz,
John Wong, 1976

but also what those forms were saying or doing to their visitors. T.S. Eliot saw that "a perception not only of the pastness of the past, but of its presence" was vital for any artist.

Designers always need to look to their clients, both to those who pay and those who will use their designs. Yet it is clearly a really difficult task for designers to know (if they can) how those users will respond. There is, parenthetically, simply no good word for those "users," which complicates how we might consider them. "Consumer" is dreadful; "spectator" is possible; "commentator" is too aloof and academic; but "audience" (suggested once by Jane Gillette) does have the advantage of realizing that the landscape is "theater," that we go there to watch and listen, to be watched, and then respond, as the play or music performs itself. It was John Ruskin who thought an interplay, an exchange, between subject and object was at the center of responding to architecture. Landscape, too. It does not—cannot—speak for itself like actors or musicians. (Indeed, many designers eschew verbal insertions.) But landscapes do mean, whether we try to understand what we see in the unmediated "wild" of forest, mountain, or desert—and also see in ourselves when we are there—or more especially when we encounter a designed space, where its elements are abstracted and epitomized, which in their turn elicit our responses.

This is a contentious territory, especially for those who value the play of forms above all. It is awkward because it is impossible to believe, in even the most democratic of worlds, that every response is plausible and worthwhile. *Quot homines, tot sententiae*—as many notions as there are people—doesn't work, at least in landscape architecture. That is properly the virtue of commentators who sift and compare responses and help us understand landscapes. There is no real way, short of endless questionnaires and interviews on sites, of acquiring responses . . . even though it is research worth pursuing. I wonder whether that is why French design teams often have a psychologist along with the usual repertoire of those who are skillful in soils, hydraulics, horticulture, lighting, and public programming—someone who possibly has insights into how people behave in places that are designed. But of course, whether analyzed or not, it is the power of Pete Walker's work—in the Tanner Fountain at Harvard, the Nasher Sculpture Center, or the National September 11 Memorial—that people bring to his designs their own receptive care.

facing page: Fountain IBM Solana Westlake, Texas, 1989

BEFORE PWP
LANDSCAPE ARCHITECTURE

Peter Walker

In PWP's 34 years of continuous practice, much has been attempt-
ed and much has been accomplished. Many difficulties and errors
have been encountered, and we have learned a lot. We have had
the tremendous advantage of growing out of The SWA Group,
which gave us a platform of experience that allowed us to begin at
a high level of professional practice. We are extremely grateful for
that experience and for the shared friendship—and friendly competition—that endures to this day. Although each firm is distinct,
we share a common history, and perhaps a good way to begin
Building Ideas is to briefly relate the highlights of that history.

In 1953 Hideo Sasaki established an office in Watertown, Massachusetts, to practice environmental design—a collaboration of
landscape architects, city and regional planners, architects, and civil
engineers. By 1957 the office had grown to six or seven professionals. Some employees were practicing designers, while others
were graduate students or recent graduates of the Harvard

16

Graduate School of Design, where Sasaki was a professor and, later, chairman of the Department of Landscape Architecture. At first the projects were mostly traditional landscape and site planning. Clients initially came from Sasaki's friends in the Harvard and MIT architectural community, but by 1959 the work had extended into resort development (Hilton Head Island), university and corporate campuses (MIT, Yale, University of Colorado at Boulder, IBM, Upjohn, Park Davis) and urban renewal (Hartford, Connecticut, and, later, San Francisco, California).

This pattern was based on Sasaki's prediction of the explosive postwar growth that would take place in transportation, education, urban renewal, and housing and his belief that larger collaborative professional offices would be required to deal with the magnitude, complexity, and urgency of that growth. This kind of practice was similar to that of the earlier Olmsted offices and in the 1950s and 1960s was known, at least within the profession, as a "corporate practice."

In 1958 the office was renamed Sasaki Walker Associates. It now comprised ten landscape architects, two architects, and a city planner. Then, in 1960 the architect Ernest Kump required that a branch of the office be opened in California in order to complete Foothill College, one of the new junior colleges mandated by California's statewide plan for higher education.

In California the new San Francisco office of Sasaki Walker Associates found a supercharged development market. In addition to an expanded education system, urban renewal was under way, the state was building a system of freeways, and the San Francisco Bay area was planning a new rapid-transit system (BART). Freeway construction had opened up land that was used to satisfy the expanding demand for housing, schools, parks, shopping centers, and medical facilities. At the time resident architects and landscape architects were preoccupied with custom suburban houses and gardens and did not initially respond to the broader dimensions of suburban growth—for example, those of the early New Town communities of Irvine and Thousand Oaks. Sasaki Walker was already thinking in these broader terms and, for the next few years, could write its own ticket. The growth was so explosive that developers didn't base their acceptance of proposals on fees, but rather on how quickly plans could be completed.

After a decade Sasaki Walker East had developed to the point where the firm could offer direct architectural services rather than work through established architectural firms. Sasaki Walker West was concerned that it would lose contracts with architectural collaborators, and so the two offices agreed that they would further define themselves, respectively, as Sasaki Dawson DeMay (SDDA) and The SWA Group. The firms separated their financial interests several years later.

By 1969 The SWA Group had grown to more than 100 employees who offered not only landscape architecture and planning, but also natural-science services, civil engineering, and outdoor graphics and communications. Along with the preponderance of housing and attendant development design work, a few projects pointed to the later work:

- Alcoa Plaza (SWA's first completely on-structure project), a city park above a two-block-long garage with sculpture by Henry Moore and Marino Marini and a fountain by Australian sculptor Robert Woodward;
- Buchanan Street Neighborhood Park, an early San Francisco redevelopment project, accomplished by closing three blocks of the street;
- Sydney Walton Park, the centerpiece of San Francisco's Golden Gateway Redevelopment area, with sculpture by François Stahly;
- Weyerhaeuser World Headquarters and Research Center (with SOM San Francisco) set in a large wooded site near the SeaTac Airport, halfway between Seattle and Tacoma, Washington;
- Concord Performing Arts Pavilion in Concord, California (with the then-young Frank Gehry office);
- IBM West Coast corporate campus in Santa Teresa, California (with McCue, Boone Tomsik Architects), the first of many IBM projects over the following 30 years;
- Crocker Plaza (with Welton Becket Architects), the first private access to a BART station in San Francisco;
- landscape master plan for Mountain View Shoreline Park, Mountain View, California, built on a municipal waste-disposal site and reclaimed San Francisco Bay shoreline;
- and, of course, the completion of Foothill College in Los Altos Hills, California.

top: Buchanan Street playground
San Francisco, California, 1973

bottom: Sydney Walton Park
San Francisco, California, with
sculpture by François Stahly, 1968

18

Weyerhaeuser World Headquarters, Federal Way, Washington, 1967

Planted stepped terraces, 2015

Plane-tree allée leading from terraced parking, 2015

Pathway through Weyerhaeuser Woods, 2015

In 1972 came a serious contraction of the economy and an oil embargo. Interest rates rose to 19 percent, and land development across the United States came to a standstill. Over the next three years The SWA Group was forced to reduce its staff by half, and the extent of its services contracted. The period of postwar expansion seemed to have come to a close.

The next ten years began with a shift of focus to a market that was less development-based as we took an interest in what has been called landscape-as-art. By 1980 our work was exploring the relationship between Miesian architecture, constructivist art, and the minimalist painting and sculpture of the 1960s. These explorations took many twists and turns and were, at times, a poor or partial fit to the types of projects and clients that presented themselves. In fact, a number were so incompatible that we were fired—a new experience that had virtually never occurred in the previous two decades.

Underlying all of these early experiments was an interest in the classical modernism of Dan Kiley and, through him, in the great European gardens of the seventeenth and eighteenth centuries. In 1956, as a graduate student at the University of Illinois at Urbana-Champaign, I had accompanied Dan on a trip to Columbus, Indiana, where he had a project under construction. The project was to become the Miller Garden, but of course at that time its future importance and beauty did not register with me. On the drive Dan asked me if I knew about the gardens of Villandry and Sceaux. I answered "no" and asked where they were. Dan went into a spirited explanation of their importance and, as I remember, an unfavorable comparison of Olmsted and Le Nôtre. He revered both but pronounced Le Nôtre as the true artistic giant. Dan had been visiting the gardens for years and described them not only in formal terms, but also in how they performed aesthetically throughout the changing seasons. He told me that I must get started visiting them as soon and as often as possible. Eighteen months later I obeyed his command and over the years have visited them dozens of times in all seasons. These visits continued throughout my years of teaching at Harvard and my art-collecting years, and they continue to this day.

top: Music pavilion
Concord, California, 1975

bottom: IBM Santa Teresa
San Jose, California, 1977

I also have a continuing dedication to Kiley's great works: the Nelson Atkins Museum, Kansas City, Missouri; La Defense, Paris, France; the MIT Great Court, Cambridge, Massachusetts; the National Gallery, Washington, D.C.; the National Bank Plaza, Tampa, Florida; Fountain Place, Dallas, Texas; and the Air Force Academy, Colorado Springs, Colorado. These projects, although quite different in many respects, combine in my mind with our early experiments and our later work to form a certain continuity of thought. I wish Dan had lived to see more of our work completed.

After The SWA Group recovered from the recession, I was personally exhausted and so, with the support of my then-partners, accepted an offer from Charles Harris to return to the Harvard Graduate School of Design to teach design as an adjunct professor. It was my first experience of full-time teaching. Part of my interest in returning to the East Coast was to live in proximity to the contemporary art I had been collecting. I obtained a loft studio in New York City's SoHo district. In 1975 SoHo was the center of contemporary art, not just in New York, but in the world. Each Saturday I would visit the many galleries and see the great painters and sculptors of the period—Donald Judd, Carl Andre, Frank Stella, and, of course, Jasper Johns, Robert Rauschenberg, and Andy Warhol.

As I began to make my first art objects, it occurred to me that the high professional quality of the art I was seeing would be difficult to master quickly. It might take years to be able to adequately express the ideas I had in mind. Later on, this frustration and some of my interesting new experiences at Harvard suggested that I might better incorporate these ideas into the craft I had learned over the last 20 years— landscape architecture, but landscape architecture expressed in a new and more experimental manner.

I have always felt that minimalism has much to offer contemporary landscape design, but in function and perhaps most of all in expression of ideas minimalist art is totally separate from landscape. Landscape design is intrinsically spatial and out-of-doors—subject to the elements and the seasons. Most of all, it is alive with a slow, steady progression from youth through maturity and, finally, decline. This progression, as we all know, is extremely difficult to control, requiring predictive knowledge and continuous loving maintenance as well as, from time to time, repair and renewal. At the very best, landscape is a tricky and problematic form of art.

top left: Shoreline Park, Mountain View, California, 1979

top right: Crocker Plaza Market Street BART Entry, San Francisco, California, 1970

bottom: Foothill College Los Altos Hills, California

left: Peter Walker William Johnson and Partners, circa 1990 – David Meyer, Tom Leader, David Walker, Jane Williamson, Tony Sinkosky, William Johnson, Doug Findlay, and Peter Walker

right: Peter Walker and Partners, circa 1999 – Peter Walker, David Walker, Doug Findlay, Paul Sieron, and Tony Sinkosky

above: Peter Walker Martha Schwartz Associates, circa 1989 – top left to right: Marta Fry, Gina Thorton, Sara Fairchild, Duane Moore, David Meyer, David Jung, Roxanne Holt, Ken Smith, Jane Hansen, Tom Leader, and Pam Palmer; bottom left to right: Rob Robold, Cathy Deino Blake, Peter Walker, Martha Schwartz, and Garth Falconer

Our current firm began in 1975 as a division of The SWA Group and was named SWA East. Over the next decade the firm morphed through a variety of partners and a number of names, including The Office of Peter Walker Martha Schwartz, Peter Walker William Johnson and Partners, and Peter Walker and Partners Landscape Architecture, to arrive at our current PWP Landscape Architecture. From the first days we began consciously to try to attract institutional clients, art museums, governments, universities, corporations, and garden owners. Such institutional clients as IBM and Weyerhaeuser, Stanford and Harvard universities, and even Central Park, had commissioned us in the past. But over the years most of our clients at The SWA Group had been development-oriented, mostly focused on "point of sale" with the landscape seen as a necessary element for selling housing, land, and commercial buildings. These projects were particularly vulnerable to major modification and removal. For years the United States has been in a period of increasing commodification, and the public landscape is, of course, no exception.

Nevertheless, throughout the last half century, a number of our designs have been cherished and cared for, even improved. As our work has matured, more institutions have employed us, and some clients have called us back to help correct failures and redesign for changing conditions. In this way we've gained valuable knowledge for our future work as well as the pleasure of witnessing the growth of individual projects. To these patrons we want to express our sincere gratitude. Another factor that has changed our practice has been repeat clients: architects, institutions, corporations, and individuals who have become friends. Repetition has increased trust, on which more advanced and experimental work can be based. Here, again, we express our deep gratitude.

Time passes, the world has broadened, and a larger number of our projects are being built in cultural contexts other than our own. Clients are seeking designers with a wider knowledge of the specific place and the cultural viewpoints of users and visitors. And so we have gained important new insights in uses, perceptions, and building practices. We have made a great many new friends, who have educated us and assisted in the successful completion of our overseas projects.

Another major change: When I first began practicing in 1956, a landscape architect was likely to be assisted by a civil engineer, an irrigation consultant, and occasionally a structural engineer or architect. Thanks in part to such pioneers as Ian McHarg, J.B. Jackson, and Frederick Steiner, landscape architects now know how important it is to have scientific and practical assistance with soils, water quality and hydraulics, drainage, horticulture, lighting, public programming, and historical and political evaluation. This new group of experts has taught the designer many things that allow for a richer depth of understanding of the context and opportunities of an individual work. All of our major projects today benefit from this extended team approach.

The three essays in *Building Ideas* discuss our work over the last 30 years. First, my friend and colleague Gary Hilderbrand explores the teaching years at Harvard and their influence on the first years of PWP Landscape Architecture. He also describes our interest in current landscape design and our attempts through Spacemaker Press to make that aspect visible to a wider cultural audience. My frequent collaborator Gina Crandell, landscape architect, writer, and teacher, has worked with us over the years at Spacemaker Press and *Land Forum* magazine. Gina is the author of *Tree Gardens: Architecture and the Forest* and *Nature Pictorialized: "The View" in Landscape History,* as well as essays and articles dealing with contemporary landscape design. She discusses the effects of our overseas work with a new group of architects. Finally, Jane Gillette, my wife and collaborator, explores the nature and direction of the firm's most recent work. Anyone who wishes to learn more about the earlier work mentioned in these essays can consult two previous publications: *Peter Walker: Minimalist Gardens* by Leah Levy (Spacemaker Press, 1997) and *Peter Walker and Partners: Defining the Craft* (ORO Editions, 2005).

top: PWP Landscape Architecture staff, 2016

bottom: View of the PWP office 2016

"Alice in Wonderland"
New York City
by sculptor José de Creeft, 1958

Raffie and the Mad Hatter, 2015

Baywood
Irvine, California, 1971

24

University Park
Irvine, California, 1966

Promontory Point
Newport Beach, California, 1975

Mariner Square
Newport Beach, California, 1970

South Coast Arts Center
Costa Mesa, California, 1991

Park at Hilton Hotel, Arts Center
Costa Mesa, California, 1991

Entry parterre, Segerstrom Opera
House, Costa Mesa, California,
1986

SPNB Headquarters
Los Angeles, California, 1974

Fashion Island Shopping Center
Irvine, California, 1968

Ethan's Glen
Houston, Texas, 1975

Fountain at Stanford University
Palo Alto, California, 1965

Bechtel Institute
University of California Irvine
Irvine, California, 1980

Upjohn World Headquarters
Kalamazoo, Michigan, 1962

Weyerhaeuser Research Center
Federal Way, Washington, 1971

Weyerhaeuser Research Center
courtyard, 1971

Cedar Riverside housing complex
Minneapolis, Minnesota, 1973

THE ROOTS OF PWP:
HARVARD AND THE DESIGN REVIVAL

Gary Hilderbrand

Tanner Fountain, an iconic 1984 work completed by Peter Walker and The SWA Group alongside the entrance to Josep Luis Sert's Science Center at Harvard University, puzzles and enchants those who pass by or choose to linger over its 159 weathered stones surrounded by asphalt paving. The project emerged as a work of significance for landscape architects—first, on its appearance, when it gave voice to a new kind of design agenda and, in 2008, when the American Society of Landscape Architects gave it their Landmark Award on its twenty-fifth anniversary. Its conceptual positioning was provocative for its time. Walker and his team appropriated a visual language from outside the discipline to redefine what a fountain on a campus could be like, and they delivered it simply, through the most essential and modest landscape materials. Its compositional strength, drawing from a radial field with apparently casual but carefully studied indifference to adjoining geometries, has been somewhat diminished by later interventions. Its creative strength carries on.

*top: Tanner Fountain viewed
from Harvard Yard*

*bottom: Tanner Fountain with
Memorial Hall beyond*

*facing page: Tanner Fountain
Harvard University, Cambridge,
Massachusetts, 1978*

Tanner Fountain's immediate public and professional reception was mixed. Although
many embraced its abstraction and the beauty of its mist and steam, there were
plenty of detractors. Contemporary landscape architectural practice and teaching in
the 1980s displayed tendencies toward a banal and conventional modernist language;
discourse about design expression, however little there was, could be said to be
dominated more by conservation or environmental planning than by intellectual or
conceptual intention. Design expression was not much discussed. Richard Weller has
noted this in his reflections on the writings of the landscape architect James Corner,
who in the 1990s aided in the shift toward a more theoretical discourse for the
field. Quoting Weller's words, I invite the reader to substitute the ordinary stones of
Walker's Tanner Fountain for the infamous but temporary lacquered bagels placed on
purple gravel by Martha Schwartz, Walker's co-conspirator at the time: "During the
mid-1980s, with Ian McHarg's call to global ecological stewardship still ringing in everyone's ears, landscape architectural discourse found itself worrying over the meaning of
a grid of bagels set out in a Boston garden. Some called it Art, others called it rubbish.
Both were wrong. The pendulum had simply swung to its counterpoint, from McHarg
and Ecology to Martha Schwartz and others seeking bold, artistic expression. The
problem was not these poles per se, but the void in between."

If Walker and Schwartz were jointly and separately pushing hard on the art side, and
at times being derided for it, they knew that what Weller identifies as the vast middle
between art-driven practice and an underconceptualized, anti-intellectual approach
to design would prove the biggest challenge. The Bagel Garden was important but
short-lived (although it shall never really die), but Tanner Fountain gained traction as
a kind of touchstone. It embodied almost a decade of intense probing by Walker and
his associates—and his students—of the ways in which the material and conceptual
practices of contemporary art could inform works of landscape architecture and
potentially redress the discipline's overriding focus on the large scale and its associated
conventional practice. The stone circle's subjective, layered image, which has been
studiously described in essays by Linda Jewell and Douglas Allen, signified an ambition
for Walker: Landscape architectural works at the project scale could be shaped by
considering the ways artists pursue beauty in their own work—through appropriation,
abstraction, iteration, and studious investigation of material qualities and meanings.

As I discussed these matters over the course of several long conversations with
Walker in the past two years, it became clear to me that his art agenda at the time
was only one among several ambitions. Across the span of more than a decade at
Harvard and then well beyond that time, his motives intertwined: He wanted to offer
an alternative to the drift toward conventional practice, move pedagogy closer to the
ways that artists and architects more typically invest in intellectual culture and theory,

top: Model of Tanner Fountain, 1976

bottom: Tanner Fountain with mist

increase the library of reference for landscape architecture, and get the work of landscape architects to be understood and discussed more critically in a broader public forum. As this book may attest, and as has been noted in earlier writings by others, successful achievement of these ambitions came through successive transformations of Walker's own thinking and practice.

The model of Tanner Fountain that Walker presented as the final proposal to Harvard was made of uniform bits of crushed colored rock with a swirl of cotton fiber representing water or steam—both, in fact. The model had only slightly more polish than the student models on the trays in Gund Hall. The adjoining Science Center, the Cambridge Street/Broadway overpass, and the fences and gates delimiting Harvard Yard were simply rendered in colored illustration board. The model was critical to Tanner Fountain's reception, but by this time, after a few years of experimentation with art precedents and reductive forms, Walker could persuade his client with practiced narratives about the sources behind the project's expressive character and exclamations about the beauty of its ephemeral mist and fog. According to Walker, Harvard's leadership at the time, including President Derek Bok and Graduate School of Design (GSD) Dean Gerald McCue, lent crucial support for an unconventional project made of rocks and asphalt and irrigation spray heads—maybe because they understood its motives or maybe because the proposal brought promise to the much-disliked and tacitly ignored asphalted space that connected the entire north campus with Harvard Yard across a barren highway overpass.

Tanner Fountain and some of Walker's and Schwartz's other works of this time shook landscape architecture's foundations and ushered in the exploration of an adventurous and sometimes audacious contemporary design language. In another visible corner, George Hargreaves' Harlequin Plaza outside Denver and his Lakewood housing subdivision in California also emblematized this shift, with slightly different emphasis. Walker's Harvard project—a far simpler and more durable work—stood on the pinpoint of a cultural shift toward a new set of references for the conceptualization of landscape. If the Bagel Garden absorbed contempt from the field's ample conservative flank for Schwartz's savvy charge against orthodox practice—and daringly paved the way for Tanner Fountain—Walker's project was accorded a more respectful reception as something groundbreaking, authoritative, and durable. As both a leading educational institution and willing patron, Harvard legitimized Tanner Fountain's place as a work of landscape architecture and helped inaugurate a disruptive turn in design culture inside its own professional school—and beyond.

DISTURBANCE

"It wasn't a revolution. Just a couple of courses that asked students to see the world differently." This is how Walker describes what he was able to do with a tiny faculty and limited resources over a few short years. Today's business experts like to speak about "disruption" as a means of deviating from norms of practice—a kind of unplanned derailment that sponsors innovation. The return to design for landscape architecture in the late 1970s and early 1980s paralleled architecture's return to language and has been well documented. This was surely one of those times when a revolution in practice paralleled an induced friction in design education. In the second decade of the twentieth century at Harvard, when Frederick Law Olmsted, Jr., moved his interest toward urban planning, a precedent was set: Curricula changed, practice reformed, and Olmsted became a leading figure in the struggle to deal with new modes of transportation and infrastructure in the American city. Landscape architecture spawned city planning as a new academic program, while its more traditional denizens retreated to practice for the wealthy. This kind of rupture happened again at the University of Pennsylvania during the 1960s with McHarg's intensive new focus on the role of science in analyzing problems of planning regional landscapes and urban expansion: New disciplines showed up at the table, curricula were revised, practices changed. In the schools, sides formed. Some teachers believed landscape architecture had a role in reconciling gigantic population shifts and environmental disasters, and they were right. Others worried that landscape architecture was abandoning its great traditions of design. Walker held a deep personal conviction that he could help the field return to a focus on design.

In the 1970s Walker and his colleagues introduced another kind of disturbance in the curriculum with the influence of artistic practice on landscape architecture. After teaching studios for two years, Walker agreed to chair the Department of Landscape Architecture in 1978 and held the position for three years. His agenda was clear: He wanted to augment what had become a dominant emphasis on land-based environmental assessments in the schools and in practice with a focus on expressive experimentation and invention in design. He pursued this strategy in three ways: revamping the beginning studio course for students entering the Master of Landscape Architecture program without a prior background in design, teaching a final-year studio based on art and design, and creating an annual non-required seminar known as "Landscape Architecture as Art." The results included the attraction of a larger and more diverse student cohort for the first professional degree; this trend foreshadowed the great strengthening of programs across the United States through the attendance of students educated in the liberal arts and humanities, a pattern that continues to benefit the field today.

top: Model of fountain for IBM Solana, Westlake, Texas, 1985

bottom: Model of parterre, IBM Solana, Westlake, Texas, 1985

MODELS

In the 1970s the department's two-year professional degree program, which brought American and international students with accredited bachelor's degrees to a two-year master's program, was the largest of its kind; the GSD's three-year program was smaller and less visible. Students and professionals who could draw convincingly—the two-year students—had the best chance for success. Attempts to teach design fundamentals, ideation, and basic drawing simultaneously to beginning design students in the three-year program perennially yielded mixed results, and weakness in representing landscape often led to perceived weakness of form or intent.

Although some remarkable tools coming out of the digital revolution have made the representation of land-based data and landscape character exhaustively robust and even luridly realistic, landscape architecture struggled in the first hundred or so years of teaching and professional practice with the problem of how to represent landscape design propositions—and the intended experience of them—with adequate means. Architects could draw the objective solids and voids of buildings convincingly since the time of Alberti's treatises, Brunelleschi's detailed instructions to masons and builders, and the invention of one- and two-point perspectival construction. But the dynamic and ephemeral qualities of landscapes defied technique and demanded special artistry—practices that took years to perfect for delineators (and, as historians and theorists tell, always came with an implicit or explicit social or political outlook that ought not be ignored).

When he became chair of the department, Walker and a few of his teaching colleagues—with few designers on the faculty at that time he borrowed regularly from the SWA office—recognized the perennial challenge that drawing landscape put to the teaching team and the students. In response, they leaned more heavily on another skill that had always been used, but not to its greatest potential—modeling landscape proposals with inexpensive cardboard and glue, wood, wire mesh, paint, and sometimes odd-looking substitutes for trees. Walker realized that working with the students who came to the program with educational and professional backgrounds in the sciences or the humanities or the arts required something other than the slow curve of learning to draw well. While the advanced design students (especially those who'd already practiced) could produce a degree of realism and believable detail in their proposals, the yet-to-be baptized first-year students had stronger appetites for abstraction and seemed less constrained by landscape conventions. This was pivotal for an instructor who was determined to accelerate a new set of precedents and practices to the forefront of design for him personally—and for the field. Modeling made the difference.

Whatever the challenges that drawing and mapping presented for landscape, models have always conveyed a palpable scaled impression of an envisioned future. Think of Vauban's massive set of fortifications models, which helped persuade the king for the vast capital required to defend the empire in its period of expansion; or consider the 1901 Senate Park Commission's enormous models of Downing's proposal for the Washington Mall and their own proposal to remake it in the version we know as the McMillan Plan. For clients and statesmen and beginning students alike, for all who cannot fully grasp space from plans, no matter how well delineated, models let the imagination penetrate into something describable, dimensional, and spatially convincing.

Above all, handcrafted models conveyed compositional, topographic, material, and spatial characteristics that could be tested and altered with relative speed and ease of technique. In the studio a student would be urged to exaggerate or reduce some factor or other and make another model. This writer remembers the combination of anxiety and motivation in the studio as Walker strolled around offering terse critiques of the work. In a final review models could be passed among critics who might hold them at eye level for enhanced viewing. In the corporate boardroom, or in the development office at Harvard, the professionally-built model would become the tool of persuasion and the display of optimistic vision. Everyone comprehends the model as a tangible substitute for reality and for the future.

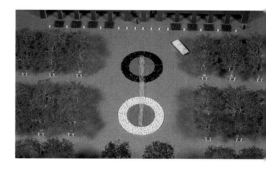

Models became the primary working method in both the first-year design studio and the final-year studio course. In his 1981 student term paper for Walker's seminar course, Fernando Magallanes (now an Associate Professor of Landscape Architecture at North Caroline State University) tells us that Walker's method was "harsh and direct." Magallanes emphasizes that Walker was "conditioning the students. He made the students draw and make models. Then he would make them draw and make more models. And then, after that, the students would do it again. It was tough love: After that first week everyone had blisters from making models. He was tough. Very, very tough."

With the advanced students Walker devised simple programs for two or three projects over the 13-week semester, starting with a catalogue of contemporary artists, sometimes undertaking projects "in the manner of" a particular artist's body of work or alternatively putting a "collection" of works on a site as a problem that merged curatorial concerns with spatial interests. In some years a roof deck was assigned; lack of soil depth wasn't considered a limitation—since plants might not be needed. The brief for the final project in these studios was often built around a commemorative program, conveniently using the proposed site reserved in Washington, D.C., for the

top: Fountain at headquarters of IBM Solana, Westlake, Texas, 1989

bottom: Model of fountain

Franklin Delano Roosevelt Memorial. Lawrence Halprin had proposed his project for the FDR Memorial long before, but in the years between Halprin's proposal and the memorial's completion, this project made for an appealing studio exercise.

The memorial program offered students something that could be powerfully meaningful through reduction and abstraction of landform, sequence, and view; that suited Walker's agenda well. During this course Walker made excursions with the students to capture immersion-in-art experience and artistic practice: galleries and artist studios in New York; museums and sculpture gardens in the corporate suburbs; and artisan foundries or factories where they could understand material assemblage or fabrication or heavy steel production. This exposure to thinkers and makers brought another kind of discussion to the curriculum and helped to broaden and deepen a critical discourse that was supplemented with readings by art critics such as Rosalind Krauss and artists, including Robert Smithson and Robert Irwin. In the studio, as in Walker's office, project models gave expression to endless discussions of form and shape, orientation and view, flatness and slope, and the scale relationships of object to field. Walker has said that his own projects with The SWA Group for Tanner Fountain and for Burnett Park in Fort Worth, Texas, and, eventually, after his departure from SWA, for the paired IBM projects of Solana Westlake and Southlake, gained from the reiterative investigations in these studios.

PWP

By now, with his professional commissions appearing in print through a Harvard supported exhibition catalog, *Peter Walker: Experiments in Gesture, Seriality and Flatness* (1990), and through frequent awards recognition in *Landscape Architecture Magazine*, Walker was influencing a generation of Harvard students and beyond. His SWA East office ran on a mix of his younger teaching colleagues and student help, and its influence was building on small but notable works. That structure was something Hideo Sasaki had perfected two decades before, precisely when Walker taught his first Harvard course, in 1959—on loan from the Sasaki Walker office. As his appetite for larger and more complex commissions increased, and as some internal tensions built around the office's relative independence from the firm's mainstream operations, Walker and Schwartz determined to move west to San Francisco in 1984 to craft a new practice that could put substantial force to larger client prospects. An evolutionary set of ventures would ultimately become what we know today as PWP, a story told in the introduction to this book and in subsequent essays. At this point Walker made time for himself and some other writers to reflect on the work from the earlier seminars and his own projects. Somebody had to do it.

34

above: Model of Library Walk University of California San Diego, La Jolla, California, 1995

facing page: Fountain in front of IBM Headquarters, South Coast Center, Costa Mesa, California, 1989

TOWARD A WIDER DISCOURSE

"There weren't any books. Nothing on design. No books on practice. Nothing on Kiley or Sasaki or even Halprin, except the books Larry had published himself. We had to start somewhere." Walker's words only slightly exaggerate the literary circumstances of landscape architecture in the 1980s: Scholarship and expository writing on landscape architecture practice were historically meager.

There were bright spots. The stellar peer-reviewed essay collections of Harvard's Dumbarton Oaks Garden Studies program featured work from scholars looking at historic landscapes, mostly focused on the European continent at this time. John Dixon Hunt's illuminating descriptive and theoretical works on garden traditions proved that a critical view of contemporary practice in landscape architecture could be built upon deep evidentiary practice in historic landscapes. Doctoral graduates in art history and the social sciences were publishing significant treatises on Olmsted's work as well as other topics. But there was little tradition of periodicals besides *Landscape Journal,* a research venue for the Council of Educators in Landscape Architecture, and the ASLA's own instrument, *Landscape Architecture Magazine*, which, after Grady Clay's editorship, had rather turned away from serious discussion about design or practice.

And so, with a business partner who knew the ropes in the publishing world, a small stable of writers, and a gifted graphic designer, Walker founded Spacemaker Press. The intrepid venture first launched a newsletter, then a set of firm monographs, a series of project studies in book form called *Landmarks,* and finally a glossy print journal, *Land Forum*. With these efforts Spacemaker began to fill the literature void and to stimulate a critical dialogue about the field.

When it came to books Spacemaker relied at first on a handy backlog of publishable subjects—the works of Walker's own firm, Schwartz's firm, and the firms of friends he knew he could call on. These were essentially real-time test cases, in which format, organization, graphic layout, printing, and distribution could be worked out with materials largely in hand; another generation of books would take longer to assemble. But Walker's sense of urgency about getting publications out there meant that a critical mass of material appeared quickly—14 issues of *Land Forum* and 24 books, including one by this author, in ten years—and the effort won the attention of the design world before printing and distribution economics made it difficult to sustain. Around the time of Spacemaker's most prolific period, in 2000, the ASLA recognized *Land Forum* with its highest mention: the President's Award of Excellence. Six years later, the *Landmarks* series was honored with an Award of Excellence.

Spacemaker brought forward designers who had little opportunity to get into print elsewhere, projects that deserved critical documentation, and issues-based commentary that had been entirely missing from view, and some notable historical studies, including Melanie Simo's benchmark edition, *100 Years of Landscape Architecture: Some Patterns of a Century*, published jointly with ASLA in 1999.

But equally important, because Spacemaker tapped a network of young teachers in schools across North America and gave them the opportunity to publish, it helped spawn a generation of writers who have continued to produce significant scholarship in the field. And as its circulation proved there was an audience for critical review, other publishing houses found fertile ground and began to commission books on practices, theories, and histories of landscape architecture. Of course there's no proof of causation. But it can be said that landscape architecture's ascendancy gained at least some traction from this frantic rush to "get it out there" and from a commitment to publishing and to discourse.

POSTSCRIPT

Tanner Fountain survives, rather like the Bagel Garden, more as an iconic image and a landmark idea than as a real landscape. Whether the rocks and mist and steam at Harvard's Science Center are renewed or not, the work lives on as a prominent touch-stone in the effort to return landscape architecture's focus to design expression.

Finally, my interest in these matters has been intensified through my own teaching for some years now with a team of gifted young teachers in the same foundational first-semester studio course at Harvard that Walker taught. Like the syllabus Walker devised 35 years ago, our course begins with the close interrogation of works that have come before us so that we may, together with the students, draw out questions of design language and grammar, relationships to sites and site systems, relationships to the body, matters of material expression, and the inexhaustible potentials of landscape phenomena: weather, microclimate, energy, growth, and maturation. We include the work of artists in these studies, just as Walker did; but we also examine both twentieth-century modernist projects and works made in our own time. I'm certain that both of these inquiries have been greatly aided by a vast increase in scholarly discussions of works that have come before. But perhaps more significantly, they've been enriched by the far wider and more diverse production of several generations of landscape architects whose own studies and practices reflect something of the world Walker was attempting to shape over these decades. That world evolved dramatically because several generations of students and practitioners learned to look outside disciplinary boundaries for motives and influences, had access to a vastly larger body of reference materials, and learned from and contribut-ed to landscape architecture's greatly enlarged discourse around design expression and its role in cultural transformation. In this reading of what a landscape architect must embrace as a body of knowledge and must accomplish in the cause of advancing the work of the discipline, parallels to Walker's own aims and ambitions over that period of time are not merely coincidental. They align, profoundly.

above: Model of Burnett Park Fort Worth, Texas, 1983

IBM Headquarters, South Coast Center
Costa Mesa, California, 1991

Roof Garden, Cambridge,
Massachusetts, 1979

Burnett Park
Fort Worth, Texas, 1983

38

left and right: Boeing Longacres Wetland Park
Renton, Washington, 1994

Principal Life Plaza
Des Moines, Iowa, 1996

Entry planting, IBM Solana
Westlake, Texas, 1989

Willows at linear pool
IBM Solana, 1989

Stylized stream, IBM Solana, 1989

left, middle, and right:
COPIA, Napa, California, 2002

Jamison Square Park
Portland, Oregon, 2006

Herman Miller
Rocklin, California, 1989

Southwest Federal Center
District Security Study
Washington, D.C., 1998

left and right: Institute for
Advanced Biomedical Research
Portland Medical Center
Portland, Oregon, 1988

left and right: Fountain
Martin Luther King Jr., Promenade
San Diego, California, 1996

REFINING THE GARDEN: 1985-2000

Gina Crandell

The variously-named practices of Peter Walker changed radically in the late 1980s and 1990s from small-scale and art-based experimental work in the United States to refined gardens in Japan and Europe that were a product of the complex nature of their circumstances. The change was unexpected. The new projects were designed for cultivated institutional clients, who were looking for work that would represent them on an increasingly global stage. PWP would collaborate with accomplished architects, engineers, consultants, and contractors with higher expectations for gardens than many of those they had worked with in the United States. Consequently PWP faced a steep learning curve.

Peter Walker was reflecting on those years of building gardens in Japan and Europe when he said, "You just don't know what you don't know." In fact, what PWP learned on these projects were eye-opening lessons in building landscapes that were very different from practice in the United States in the early 1980s.

top: IBM Solana
Westlake, Texas, 1989

bottom: IBM Solana Sales Center

In Japan and Europe, for example, the level of building craft that was expected and at hand for construction was remarkable. The availability of plants in nurseries was far more specialized than in the United States. Building in these countries also meant working with different systems of competition, authorization, and procurement. Together these demands broadened and concentrated PWP's knowledge of landscape architecture.

At the same time, the new projects presented PWP with a fresh opportunity to apply the thinking of the previous decade. To these international projects PWP would bring a mature modernism, a renewed respect for the classic gardens of Le Nôtre, and concepts interpreted from minimalist artists such as Donald Judd, Carl Andre, and Frank Stella that Walker had already translated into small experimental projects. But these new projects would be in the context of large and complex sites in different cultures.

We're familiar with many of these projects. We've seen the trunks of closely planted birches in the courtyard at Novartis. We've seen the lighted rocks and the raked gravel, the perfectly formed moss and stone hills, the misting and aerating fountains, and the polished logs in PWP's Japanese gardens from the 1990s. We've recognized that the overlapping grids of hedges and gravel at the Hotel Kempinski in Munich allude to seventeenth-century French parterres. We're quite familiar with the experiments that preceded them, the clay pots and mirrors on the rooftop in the Back Bay and certainly the Tanner Fountain. We even know the images of Carl Andre's floor pieces, which enticed us into an understanding of how one might translate sculpture into landscape architecture. But can we imagine what it was actually like to design a Japanese garden for a Japanese client interpreted from a Carl Andre floor piece?

There's a lot of luck in success. Walker has had his share. As a student he joined Hideo Sasaki just when Sasaki was inventing the large multidisciplinary office. In his first jobs at Sasaki while working on early suburban corporate headquarters, he was introduced to the most Miesian of architecture offices, Skidmore in Chicago. He opened the West Coast office of Sasaki Walker Associates in 1958, just when California was leading the country's development boom. At that time he climbed a steep learning curve to scale up to very large fast-track projects for California developers in which the primary impetus was the speed at which the work could get built. When the postwar prosperity slowed in the 1970s, Walker headed back to Harvard to teach and experiment with ideas, in particular exploring his interests in minimalism. That small office, SWA East, was fired many times in its attempts to translate ideas from art into landscape. But in 1989, through the luck of a connection and a fluke, the

office was given free rein to build a huge, really advanced industrial park for IBM in Solana, Texas—even though the office had never worked on such a large project before. The IBM Texas project led to a commission for IBM in Japan, in an industrial redevelopment area outside Tokyo called Makuhari. The IBM Makuhari project opened the phase of PWP's work in which the collaboration with cosmopolitan architects was combined with serious institutional clients.

Art Hedge, the vice-president of IBM who was responsible for initiating global building projects, was an advocate for design excellence. In the late 1980s and 1990s he was inspired to house the corporation in gardens and buildings that would express the company's inventiveness and cultural sophistication. For the designers, first in Texas and then in Japan, this meant that the client was both open to ideas and willing to support them.

It wasn't just the vice-president of IBM who had high expectations for the landscape. So did the architect IBM hired. Yoshio Taniguchi had studied in Japan and in the United States. His father had participated in the modern architecture movement in Japan and served as architect to the Emperor before the war. Taniguchi had learned from his father (and from his culture) to treat each project with great care. Consequently, Taniguchi's office embodied a model of practice that was different from the large corporate office of the typical American architect. His was a small office of 10 to 15 people who worked on only a few projects each year. PWP was also a small office at that time and even today maintains this model—fewer than 30 people working on a small number of projects at any one time.

Along with music, painting, and poetry, gardens have long been among the most revered arts in Japan, and while lovers of Western gardens have appreciated representational stone or bronze sculpture, lovers of East Asian gardens have admired rocks and trees altered by natural processes. Before the twelfth century both the practice of erecting rocks to be viewed from a distance and creating spaces in Imperial gardens simply of white sand or gravel had become established. The fifteenth-century Zen Buddhist garden, Ryoan-ji in Kyoto, composed of 15 stones in an enclosed gravel plain, is not a representation of something else, real or mythical. Instead it is an intellectual composition of unaltered stones in space. There may be no explanation for the 5 / 2 / 3 / 2 / 3 organization of stones at Ryoan-ji, and that may be precisely the point. If something simply represents something else, there is no mystery to contemplate. Ideas relating to inexplicable phenomena and the value of "emptiness" connected with Walker's interest in minimalism and inspired PWP's gardens in Japan.

top: IBM Solana Town Center

bottom: IBM Solana Sales Center

top: *Model of IBM Japan Headquarters Makuhari, Japan, 1991*

bottom: *The computer punch card at IBM Makuhari*

When Taniguchi asked PWP to design a Japanese garden for the new IBM headquarters in Makuhari, Walker asked him what he meant by a Japanese garden. Taniguchi said: carefully made and intellectually based. He did not want a flabby representation of nature adjoining his building because he saw the garden as a work of art. Most American architects in the 1980s—and most American landscape architects as well—carried around ideas that landscape was a setting for the building and should pretend to look as if it were natural and not designed. Indeed, it might be worth thinking about American culture in the 1980s. Back then, cities were not desirable; public landscapes, even Central Park, were largely unkempt; and there were no such things as aged cheese, fresh roasted coffee, artisanal chocolate, craft beer, and local food. Gardens were considered little more than neutral grounds for buildings rather than opportunities for objective design statements that engaged contemporary culture. Even an art project like the Marlborough Roof Garden, with mirrors representing water and diminishing clay pots representing Le Nôtre's forced perspective, was temporary. But in Japan PWP found a changing scene. The pastoral calm of Olmsted did not apply to the corporate courtyard. The fast turnover of developer projects was quite unlike the investment in projects that would characterize work for long-term institutional clients. The venerated Japanese sense of craft and the appetite for a strong concept necessitated professional innovation and a transformation of all of PWP's earlier work.

At Makuhari, in order to establish a formal vocabulary, PWP paired the idea of the (now obsolete) computer punch card, in which pattern corresponds with information, with local materials common in Japanese gardens: water, bamboo, stone, moss, rock, evergreen shrubs, jade pebbles, gravel, and willows. To present their concept PWP took another innovative leap from past practice. They had seen in the first half of the twentieth century how professionals had moved from just drawing plans (if they were drawing at all) to the novel sketches that enabled Thomas Church to communicate directly with builders. But neither was suitable for communicating the abstract sculptural concept PWP was to present to Taniguchi. In the late 1970s Walker did experimental work with his students translating ideas from sculptural maquettes into landscape models. As a result the model was practically reinvented as the means of communicating three-dimensional ideas in landscape. From that experience PWP polished the technique by building many skillfully crafted models that expressed the strength of their concepts spatially.

The model proves particularly appropriate for explaining the garden at Makuhari. Following the Japanese tradition of viewing the garden from a distance and from above, the actual garden is seen from the skywalk that Taniguchi designed parallel to the building. Walking from the train station to the building entrance, pedestrians look into a series of courtyards unfolding below: a gravel island of willow trees set within a pool, a garden of hedges, a bamboo plantation surrounding stone benches, a pond of water lilies, a gravel courtyard with a giant stone that hovers weightlessly above the ground. Each courtyard presents only a few materials in an orthogonal composition. These gardens surely do not imitate traditional Japanese gardens, but they certainly reference them.

One of the issues PWP faced in scaling up from the small experimental garden to the large corporate garden was the necessity of incorporating practical infrastructure without interfering with the conceived organization. At Makuhari humble practicalities, such as driveways and visitor parking (which often overwhelm the best of intentions) take a rectangular form perceived as a courtyard with a circular stone plinth. This full integration of practical amenities into the garden erases the usual division between engineering and art. The largest gesture at Makuhari exemplifies this idea: A glass-encased "data" line cuts through all the courtyards, parallel to the skywalk and lighted at night, a formal element that at the same time invisibly incorporates utilities into the garden, again upending functional divisions.

The ground plane, entirely built above structure, is flat, and gravel is predominant. Japanese sand or gravel gardens may be thought of as "empty." But this condition of emptiness brings sensory and intellectual experience to the moment and holds it there. It is the art of the void, the calm that creates notice. This idea is not limited to Japanese gardens. It is also present in minimalist art, which broke away from representation to refresh experience; it required precise dimensions and demanded attention yet without source or tradition. By contrast, when forms of art and architecture become broadly accepted—for example, the naturalistic garden—they tend to become increasingly generalized both in sensory effect and thought. PWP reverses this degenerative process with rigorous consideration and a restrained palette. The emptiness of the garden at Makuhari is designed to evoke a silence that intensifies spatial experience. The opportunities offered to PWP to design gardens in Japan brought ideas from Japanese gardens and minimalist art together with a freshness and specificity that could only have happened in the 1990s.

above: Details of the computer punch card at IBM Makuhari

PWP endeavors to make natural processes visible through the artifice of building projects. At Makuhari living things are made visible through contrast: Everything is orthogonal except for living things (and the giant stone that some would argue was once alive). The boldly constructed, flat, and largely stone courtyards intensify the perception of living forms: leaning bamboo canes, mounds of moss, hanging

top: Train Station Plaza and Museum Marugame, Japan, 1991

middle: Toyota Municipal Museum of Art, Toyota City, Japan, 1995

bottom: Fountain at Toyota Museum

facing page: Oyama Training Center Oyama, Japan, 1993

willow branches, and textured evergreen hedges. The ephemeral patterns of light and shadow are amplified by the stone surfaces, which act as a bright screen upon which the dark shapes move. In this as in the other Japanese projects, Taniguchi introduced PWP to skilled Japanese contractors who had experience with local soils, plants, and drainage—for example, an electrical engineer who consulted on the glass encasement that incorporates utilities into the garden.

PWP worked with Taniguchi Associates on other projects in Japan in the 1990s. Marugame Plaza is designed to serve the train station for Marugame City. Pedestrians may walk in any direction on the visually flat surface that is objectified by black asphalt and white cobblestone bands and partially built over structure. But it is the coming and going from the train station that is indicated by a line of identical artificial rocks forming a spiral of seating in front of an outdoor stage for displaying sculpture. PWP proposed lighted rocks because most employees arrive for work before and return home after daylight. The first lighted rocks PWP designed were for Oracle in Redwood City, California. But the engineers at Oracle were offended by their artificiality and had them removed. They may have been welcomed in Japan because, as Walker explains, even contemporary Zen monks were using fake rocks.

For the Toyota Museum of Art, the client was the mayor of Toyota City, who himself had a collection of art, was passionate about teahouses, and wanted a museum for the city. As part of the project PWP designed two gardens for sculpture: a checkerboard-patterned space of gravel and grass panels for monumental sculpture and wide bands of grass and ground cover crossed by lines of dawn redwood trees for human-scaled sculpture. PWP was challenged to consider new approaches. The contractors and architects asked them to keep working until they got it right. Walker says it was like practicing music. For example, the mayor wanted a fountain. Since PWP did not want a kinetic fountain that might compete with the sculpture, they designed a large shallow pond and then invented an air fountain in the surface of the pond. Much like a Carl Andre floor piece, flatness was emphasized, although it was amplified to landscape scale.

Built atop a large four-story building above an existing rail yard, the plaza at Saitama-Shintoshin Station, located north of Tokyo, is probably the flattest on earth—with the idea of flatness fully integrated into the natural processes of the site. Rainwater drains directly through the plaza to an "earth room" of designed soils that irrigate the plaza's grove of 220 zelkova trees. The owners, the Saitama Prefectural Government, needed the project to serve as a pedestrian core for transit connections as well as residential, retail, and office space. PWP won a competition with OHTORI and NTT Urban

above: Nishi Harima Conference
Center, Nishi Harima, Japan, 1993

Development Company with the proposal to site the plaza on the topmost surface of the glass building. The construction detailing and installation supervision provided by the landscape architects of OHTORI, NTT UD, and Japanese landscape architect Yoji Sasaki demonstrated the highest level of craft in creating the extreme flatness and drainage. PWP learned how the permeability of a ground plane could be expressed on its surface and would later incorporate the idea into other projects, particularly the Nasher Sculpture Center and the National September 11 Memorial.

In 1990 PWP was hired by the Hyogo Prefectural Government and collaborated with Arata Isozaki and others to create a master plan for a new town, Nishi Harima Garden City, in a mountainous interior valley of Japan that had been stripped of much of its forest. In the interior courtyard of Isozaki's Center for Advanced Science and Technology, PWP designed a garden with a quiet power reflective of traditional Japanese meditation gardens injected with a certain detached humor. Two giant, steepsided cones—one of precisely cut spiraling stone, the other of moss—appear like distant mountains and infuse the space with a surrealistic scale. The quiet esteem that is accorded to stone in this project reflects a merger of Japanese tradition and PWP's minimalist refinement. Lines of black granite, polished on the surface and rusticated on the sides, intersect with a line of flat-topped fieldstones on a plane of raked gravel. In the lower stream pond, the peaks of a line of dark fieldstones break the water surface above a band of white cobblestones. In the Circular Park, individual stones fit tightly together without mortar to form a dome that is lighted from within at night. To more fully express the diverse character of stone, a semicircle of fake standing stones hulks above the dome and glows at night.

During the time that PWP was working in Japan, they were also working on projects in Germany, a country with a landscape history and design practice also differing widely from the American example. Indeed, PWP found that working in Germany in the 1990s had many parallels with working in Japan. For one thing, PWP found a similarly deep appreciation for the design of public spaces in institutional clients as well as in the international architects with whom they were collaborating.

Michael Pollan has nicely summarized the differences between American and European conceptions of nature in his book *Second Nature*: Americans take their bearings from the wilderness, the unknown they encountered just centuries ago, shortly before it was plundered for resources. By contrast Europeans, with a much longer history of living on the land, take their bearings from the garden. Accordingly, the American vision leads to laissez faire, a desire to let nature go its own way, while the European vision requires constant care and active participation in the temporal and ephemeral qualities of gardens.

49

In the 1990s PWP collaborated on numerous projects with architect Helmut Jahn, who grew up in Germany but opened his office in Chicago. Jahn brought a European sensibility to landscape—an appreciation for natural processes through their interaction with people in the wild, in agriculture, and in the city. He had a particular appreciation for playfulness and invention. And he wanted the landscape to relate to the building—and then go beyond that. The projects during this period were largely in Germany, and therefore PWP had access to Jahn's consultants and a very high level of German craftsmanship. The design freedom of PWP's projects with Jahn expanded the scale and materiality of Walker's ideas of flatness, patterning, and transparency as well as the seamless integration of infrastructure.

Walker's experimental work on formalism had led to using patterns on the ground to make the objectivity of a flat surface more present. Referring to Andre's floor pieces, Walker explained how hard it is to make flatness apparent: "You can put down patterned paving and all you have is patterned paving. But if you learn how to really flatten and contain it, then you have presence." Walker combined an interest in triangles that had come from Frank Stella's paintings with an appreciation of Le Nôtre's parterres. It was like making paintings on the ground, which in the case of the Hotel Kempinski, in the Munich Airport Center, lay above underground structure. Overlapping grids that angle away from the front of the hotel produce triangular panels within square hedges. At the Sony Center in Berlin the flatness of the plaza surface is created by a pattern of crisscrossing bands of light gray steel plates, black cobblestones, and dashed blue-glass insets that reach from edge to building edge. Here the flatness is further solidified by contrast—a rupture in the ground plane where a reflecting pool cantilevers over the exposed lower level.

Glass dominated the surfaces of Jahn's buildings, and to their collaboration Walker brought his own interests in transparency, particularly the possibilities of the ambiguity between inside and out. Their shared interests in transparency led to intense discussions and numerous applications. At the Hotel Kempinski the courtyard is both inside and out, covered and exposed. Jahn's transparent walls dematerialize the building, while PWP's tall and shallow glass structures (housing fake geraniums) cut right through the building to the outside. These early applications of transparency expanded PWP's vocabulary of designed materials and transformed materials that seemed solid into ones with all kinds of openings. At the Sony Center PWP punched holes in the stainless steel that formed benches to open them to air and light. In the paving, wide bands of stainless steel were punctured with a pattern of diagonal cutout lines. At the Principal Mutual Life project in Des Moines, Iowa, the mist fountain and lantern were constructed of steel plates with a tracery of large openings that were

*above: Saitama-Shintoshin Plaza
Saitama, Japan, 2000*

50

top: Model of Sony Center
Berlin, Germany, 1999

middle: Pool from theater lobby

bottom: Pool at ground level

permeated by daylight or at night by artificial lighting. All of these designs originated from discussions about transparency. PWP had never interacted with architects this intensely.

These forays into transparency along with ideas of patterning and flattening, particularly on increasing numbers of projects built above structure, led unexpectedly to a new conception of the ground plane as a skin above and below which all kinds of functions were operating, functions that design strategies could express. At the Sony Center the bands of stainless steel paving, perforated with cutout patterns, were also operational grates that held all of the utilities and accommodated drainage in their interstitial spaces. These early designs incorporating utilities into the material framework of a garden would have lasting ramifications for PWP. For example, Sydney Olympic Park integrated water filtration and soil remediation into formal strategies: The waste materials were combined in 90-foot-high ziggurat hills placed at the entrances and from which stretches of the 1,600-acre park could be viewed. At the Nasher Sculpture Center in Dallas electrical pull boxes, low-voltage lighting transformers, power outlets, irrigation-valve boxes, irrigation-hose connections, purified-water connections, and speakers are housed in linear stone seating plinths that also serve as sculpture platforms. At the National September 11 Memorial the linear framework itself is a system that generates allées of trees above soil trenches and, alternately, underground maintenance corridors for drainage and irrigation emphasized by bands of stone carrying stainless steel drains.

PWP was introduced to Jahn's glass consultant, Jamie Carpenter, whose superior knowledge of glass applications opened even more possibilities for experimentation. PWP was able to propose ideas they didn't know how to construct because they were working with such experienced consultants. In 1992 when PWP proposed a cantilevered glass pool at the Sony Center, they didn't yet know how they would build it. Jahn's office would help figure out how to do it, and the Sony fountain is evidence of innovation and expertise not found in the United States at the time. At the Principal Mutual Life project Jahn's consultants helped figure out how to design a misting fountain in which the mist doesn't blow away or get people all wet. Clients, architects, and contractors with a desire for excellence bracketed this phase of PWP's practice and were willing to invent whatever was necessary to achieve it.

In 1999 PWP began work on the Novartis Headquarters campus in Basel, Switzerland. The president of Novartis was looking for a way to transform the former industrial area into a contemporary, secure campus where casual meetings among scientists would propel research. Historic campuses, such as Jefferson's Lawn at the University of Virginia, were designed for social interaction between faculty and students. But most campuses have long since outgrown opportunities for collaborative encounters. Novartis was dedicated to the idea that the civic space structuring the campus and its many special gardens should be conducive to scientific conversation. PWP's design for the civic space was founded on a series of very basic ideas involving scale and materials. It was about using the right trees and the right paving and getting the proportions just right. All of the little pieces must fit together to make a very special place.

The Novartis experience in Switzerland was different from working in Japan or Germany. Novartis is one of the Medicis of the twenty-first century. Every part of the campus was precious, and all work had to receive approval from a committee that met frequently to discuss design progress. Buildings were treated separately from the civic space and gardens. The Swiss love nature and modernism. They are very intellectual and demanding of restraint. Perhaps as a result, PWP's work at Novartis is the most honed, simplified, and classic of anything they've done in Europe. The civic space that PWP designed satisfies humble needs—curbs and gutters, street signs and trees—in a demanding design climate. For example, PWP spent months refining the question of how a metal fence would be made. The stairway underneath the Serra sculpture is their best work in concrete: The finish is perfectly smooth, nothing is cracked, and the form skillfully changes direction. One of the gardens, the Birch Courtyard, is a magical place. The built materials are so perfectly refined that the trees and the light, by contrast, sparkle with life. The Novartis campus is a 50-year project. Some of the trees PWP has planted in the civic space will structure new streets that are still under development. In five decades they will be mature, and who knows what new drugs will have been invented.

Local practices of landscape architects have grown in Japan, Germany, and Switzerland in recent years, and the projects PWP designed there in the 1990s have become precedents for new work. These projects represent an important phase of PWP's work, and they also represent an important learning curve for the profession of landscape architecture. We now have a portfolio of freshly conceived large-scale projects with refined vocabularies that speak to their particular cultural and environmental locales. We now have specialized consultants for building at a technical capacity that was simply not available 30 years ago. We now have a range of precedents for incorporating engineering infrastructure into the design conception of a landscape. We may have reached the time when the idea of translating minimalist art into landscape is something of the past. But the legacy remains. We have a far deeper understanding of how a landscape can become classic when the art of its own time is interpreted and precisely clarified. There will continue to be contexts where objectivity and restraint are the most beautiful responses to particular places. This was the case in seventeenth-century France and in Makuhari and Basel at the end of the twentieth ... and it will be so again in landscapes committed to refinement in the twenty-first century.

top: Novartis Headquarters Basel, Switzerland, sculpture by Richard Serra, 2005

bottom: Main street Novartis Headquarters

Bayer Headquarters
Leverkusen Germany, 2002

left and right: Shanghai Taipingqiou Park
Shanghai, China, 2002

Marugame Train Station Plaza and Museum
Marugame, Japan, 1992

left and right: Forum, Novartis Headquarters
Basel, Switzerland, 2005

Center for Clinical Sciences
Research, Stanford University
Palo Alto, California, 2002

left and right: Clark Center
Stanford University, 2003

Model of Kempinski Hotel
Munich, Germany, 1994

left and right: Kempinski Hotel, 1994

Novartis Headquarters
Basel, Switzerland, 2005

left and right: President's Court, Novartis
Headquarters, Basel, Switzerland, 2005

Model of Sony Center
Berlin, Germany, 2000

left, middle, and right: Deutsche Post
Headquarters, Bonn, Germany, 2002

54 BUILDING IDEAS

Jane Gillette

We can date the beginning of a new period at PWP Landscape
Architecture to 1997, when Tony McCormick of HASSELL, an
architecture, urban design, and landscape architecture firm in
Sydney, Australia, invited Peter Walker to join the design team for
the 2000 Olympic Games. Keeping an eye on budgets, schedules,
and outcome, McCormick managed some 15 consultants who
helped transform one of the most polluted sites in the world into
a usable—and beautiful—green environment. During the course
of this project Walker participated in meetings during which he
watched McCormick maximize the use of specialists in soils, horticulture, environmental management, lighting and solar energy,
reforestation, landfill and geotechnical engineering, and irrigation and drainage, to name but a few. "I didn't quite know what
we were doing," recalls Walker. "We'd never used any of these
people. Occasionally we'd have a soil specialist and occasionally
we'd have somebody who could calculate floods. But we'd never
used anyone to do specialized planting or even regular planting.

top: Peter Walker and Renzo Piano at the site of Nasher Sculpture Center (a former parking lot), Dallas, Texas

middle: Dr. Robert Moon supervising tree planting at William P. Clements Jr. University Hospital, Dallas, Texas

bottom: Conard Lindgren inspecting planting soil, VMware Headquarters Palo Alto, California

We'd talk to the nursery men, we'd talk to tradespeople." To some degree this is exaggeration because PWP (under its various names) had used consultants. They were, however, usually hired and supervised by the European and Japanese architects who initiated many of the PWP projects in the 1980s and 1990s.

Of course consultants had existed in the United States for decades. For example, Ian McHarg and other early environmentalists in landscape architecture had pointed out their role, assuming somewhat unrealistically that they would come out of university landscape architecture programs. And firms in the United States had used consultants, although at a regional scale—for example, in mapping. Consultants were seldom if ever called in on small-scale individual projects. For the most part, landscape architects relied on themselves. Conard Lindgren, a partner at PWP who spends much of his time interacting with consultants, remembers how the firms he worked for in the 1980s did everything in-house: "We had our own survey equipment. We did our own irrigation design, our plant and paving designs. We worked with the skill set we'd already learned . . . or could teach ourselves." This way of going about things involved a lot of trial and error. As time passed, the use of a structural engineer and an irrigation consultant became pretty standard practice, the specialists contributing first and foremost to efficiency.

Eventually consultants began to be hired at project scale, especially by the larger firms. For PWP the first project in which the role of consultants proved all-important was the Nasher Sculpture Center in Dallas, begun in 1999. At first, attention focused on the building by architect Renzo Piano, then shifted to the outdoor gallery, which would be the location of a few permanent sculptures along with changing exhibits of some 20 to 30 pieces from the roughly 600 in the Nasher collection. This constant change meant that the garden needed a special soil that would hold up under the stress of trucks as well as heavy works of art. It would also have to drain perfectly without catch basins in order to create the flat plane necessary for properly displaying sculpture. And it would have to sustain the growth of specimen trees and turf grass in both sun and shade. This soil—which Mr. Nasher fondly called "million-dollar dirt"—was created by soil specialist Chuck Dixon, the planting of specimen trees was supervised by Dr. Robert Moon, and the fountains were designed by Dan Euser. All three consultants worked on later PWP projects, Euser and Dixon on the National September 11 Memorial.

PWP was not alone in increasing the use of consultants, who flourished profession-wide as ecological regulations became more pervasive and landscape architects saw how much more the consultants knew about these issues than they did. Likewise consultants saw a growing market in landscape architects and by the 1990s were becoming more numerous and more specialized. "Consultants evolved within their own fields," explains Lindgren. "Say they used to run labs that did the soil testing. They'd sell the lab and open their own soil-consulting business."

57

Where, then, did they come from, these consultants? Over the years PWP tried out any number and stuck with a few, as the reader can see from the lists in the back of this book. If we look at a small sample from the PWP files, we learn that consultants are not, by and large, landscape architects. Although there are exceptions. For example, fountain designer Dan Euser started off as a landscape architect "doing lots of technical stuff" for a large company in Canada: "When a fountain came along on any project, I was involved with it." He left after 15 years and did fountain design for another company until 1997, when he started his own business, Dan Euser Waterarchitecture. Likewise, Stuart Pittendrigh, creator of the remarkable bush planting for Barangaroo Reserve, studied, first, mechanical engineering and, then, landscape architecture and horticulture at a variety of Sydney institutions. He worked worldwide for a number of companies and now has his own, Norcue.

Most PWP consultants learned their specialty from some combination of scientific/academic education and hands-on involvement. For example, Dr. Robert Moon, horticulturalist for Nasher and the University of Texas projects, has a Master of Science degree in Horticulture, a Ph.D. in Crop Science, and his own company, Dr. Robert E. Moon & Associates. Consultant for a host of PWP projects, John Swallow, who holds a Ph.D. in Organic Chemistry from MIT, is principal and founder of Pine & Swallow Environmental, a practice emphasizing soil chemistry, environmental conditions for plant growth, site rehabilitation, and tree planting techniques. Swallow started a tree nursery when he was 12 years old: "From a young age I always questioned the composition of everything, including roots and soil and organic matter, the soil critters, and all that compose nature's web." Soil scientist Simon Leake, whose expertise has been critical to Sydney Olympic Park and Barangaroo Reserve (where he created soil out of excavated rock), studied agricultural science at the University of Sydney, majoring in soil science, then set up his own laboratory and office, SESL. Charles Dixon, devisor of the "million-dollar dirt" and soils engineer for the National September 11 Memorial, has a Master of Science degree and did post-degree study in agronomy and soil microbiology; he gained experience designing soils for various sports venues, including golf and thoroughbred

top: Announcement of Memorial competition selection, New York City, 2005: left to right — Peter Walker, Michael Arad, Governor George Pataki, and Mayor Michael Bloomberg

bottom: Dan Euser at full-scale fountain mock-up, Richmond Hill, Ontario, Canada, 2005

racing, and has his own company, C.R. Dixon & Associates. Paul Cowie, arborist for the National September 11 Memorial, studied natural resources management at Rutgers University, concentrating on forestry and timber management; he then worked for a small tree-service company before establishing his own consulting business. Architectural lighting designer Paul Marantz studied architectural history at Oberlin College, stage design and lighting at Case Western Reserve University and Brooklyn College; in 1971 he formed his own firm, which has developed into Fisher Marantz Stone, creators of "Tribute in Light" and the lighting for the National September 11 Memorial.

And then there are those who've come by their knowledge in a hands-on fashion. Barangaroo consultant Troy Stratti's parents were earthmoving contractors who excavated "large deep holes for high-rise buildings through the 1970s and 1980s." Troy enjoyed working in the family business during his school breaks and incorporated his first company when he was 19 years old. He took a different approach from his parents and built his reputation by contracting and extracting sandstone. Troy also invented the Stratti rocksaw, which aided in the excavation of the beautiful sandstone we see at Barangaroo Reserve.

And how do landscape architects find these consultants? At first PWP hired many via Tony Sinkowski, PWP consultant and at that time one of the partners in charge of supervising construction. According to Lindgren, some consultants initially came to their attention through lawsuits: "They were on the other side," and it seemed wise to learn what they were all about. Today consultants are less dramatically discovered in trade publications, for example, in the lists at the end of articles in *Landscape Architecture Magazine*. They often speak at conferences and trade shows. And word of mouth is all-important. Consultants do not, however, tend to market themselves aggressively, perhaps because, as Lindgren suggests, many like to "keep at a safe distance where they can give you your input and not assume all the responsibility."

Responsibility is definitely an issue in using consultants. To some degree their pervasive use makes the landscape architect sound like the movie director who chooses and guides all those specialists listed in the trailer at the end of the movie. Responsibility for the final product—on many levels—sticks to the landscape architect as it does to the director, who is, above all else, the person in charge. "Consultants can provide their licensing stamps on all their work, but ultimately we own the documents. So, if they're wrong we're wrong," explains Lindgren. This means that the landscape architect takes legal responsibility. And, equally important, the landscape architect is in charge of paying the consultants for their input with money that usually comes out of the fee paid to the landscape architect. Hence, landscape architects have an incentive to get the client to appreciate the value of consultants so they will pay extra for their use. Clients may require persuasion. For example, Walker remembers that in the old days certain things in the project would have to go wrong before the client saw the need for a specialist. And in the old days when the firm was doing development projects, even failure didn't count for much because the client was quickly going to sell the project, failure and all. Now, when clients are, on the whole, building for themselves, they are more likely to see specialized consultants as a source of added value and security.

The best consultants know how things work. They know how to make things better and easier. They provide outside information—for example, how other design firms are doing it, whatever "it" is. But the landscape architect has to keep a close eye on things. Responsibility for this aspect of the projects frequently falls heavily on what could metaphorically be called the assistant directors, the members of the firm who devote themselves to project management. But at PWP the ultimate responsibility for legality, money, management, and much more lies in the hands of partner Douglas Findlay. To indulge in another metaphor, he is the chief cook and bottle-washer and, along with Walker, the originator of all business policy. "As everyone knows," says Walker, "Doug is the heart of our firm." He spends his days on the telephone and computer negotiating with clients, government agencies, and, of course, consultants. In the metaphor of the movie business Doug is the producer, the one who stands behind everything. And, as Doug stresses, he is always working, in his own way, for the ultimate success of the design.

In the PWP office you simply can't overstress the importance of design, which goes well beyond issues of legality, money, and management. And in this regard, Lindgren stresses, you have to pick consultants you can go down the road with. You have to decide "if you're going to go with this guy's style or that guy's style. Both of them are going to deliver a good project, but in different ways." And those different ways of doing things can crucially affect the design of the project because the best consultants do not shun the aesthetic. For one thing, when there are differences of opinion on the design team, they can serve as important referees. They can confirm and criticize: This will work, that won't. And they can shake things up.

59

top: Michael Arad and Peter Walker in discussion at Memorial site New York City, 2005

bottom: Ron Vega, and workers, at planting of last tree at the Memorial, 2015

At Barangaroo Reserve, Sydney, Australia, 2014 — back left to right: Simon Leake, Troy Stratti, Peter Walker, Stuart Pittendrigh, James Restuca, and Peter Gallert; front left to right: Kieron Little and Sam Stratti

top: Bob Nation, Barangaroo Delivery Authority design director, and David Walker at Barangaroo, 2015

bottom: Former Australian Prime Minister Paul Keating and New South Wales Premier Mike Baird at Barangaroo Reserve opening, 2015

Put five experts together in a room with a few designers and everyone may be inspired to all sorts of new things by the mingling of various areas of expertise. According to Walker, this is one of the ways in which the very best consultants inspire creativity. "We're always looking for people who have a creative urge in addition to their expertise," consultants who are artists and generate ideas, formal ideas. For example, Walker has the highest praise for Stuart Pittendrigh's bush landscape, specific not just to Australia, but to Sydney in particular, and critical to the way the headland looks. If it weren't for Pittendrigh's planting Barangaroo wouldn't look like a headland. And then there's the shoreline. From the outset PWP wanted to use large sandstone blocks quarried from the site. A consultant said no. But quarryman Troy Stratti said yes, and Stratti knows virtually everything there is to know about sandstone, including the breaks in the stone, the angles that show how the headland was formed. Ultimately it was his advice that transformed the project. "He's an expert, a master stone mason, but he's also an artist," says Walker. "Troy was able to do things we couldn't imagine." In much the same tone Walker refers to Dan Euser, whose design for the fountains at the National September 11 Memorial assured that they use relatively little water, thereby saving energy and hence money and thus making the Memorial feasible. But in addition to their economic value those thin streams of water are one of the things that make the waterfalls beautiful.

To the nonprofessional it might seem that consultants are more necessary to a large site than to a small one, to a polluted site than to one built on pure, clean concrete. But everyone at PWP seems to agree that, large or small, dirty or clean, every site requires consultants, especially from specialties that are clearly related to environmental issues. Over the past 15 years PWP has continued to practice as landscape architects have traditionally done— providing the surrounds for architect-directed projects. But, as you can see in the following project descriptions, many of their most important projects are not building-dominated. These landscapes are saying something in and of themselves. Consider two of the most important. Both are on large sites with terrible environmental issues. Both have complex bureaucratic clients. Both are designed for extensive public use. Both are memorials: The National September 11 Memorial in New York City commemorates the victims of the terrorist attacks; Barangaroo Reserve celebrates the wife of the Aboriginal leader in 1788, the date of the first European arrival. Both projects are expressions of ecological processes: The National September 11 Memorial is

in essence a fountain, a cycle of rainwater on a green roof; Barangaroo is a re-created headland on the former site of a container port. Both are projects in which consultants were indispensable.

Historically the most memorable landscapes have been created within cultural milieus that support a complex intertwining of belief and need. For example, English pastoral landscapes depended in part on a client class who had studied the classics, made the Grand Tour, and owned a lot of land. Whatever their architectural function, Zen gardens were created within a religious context. For example, Ryoan-ji is a beautiful designed landscape that represents nothing, a physical expression of the nonrepresentative status of the world, an idea with a long history in Buddhist religious thought. Or consider the context of André Le Nôtre, who served a court that needed to stretch its political control to the horizon while it controlled the aristocrats lounging around the premises. What wonderful solutions do we see at Versailles in the extended views created by false perspectives and those essentially manageable allées! Control has been made to look inevitable as, once again, formal solutions flow from a complicated mix of belief systems and practical necessities. It may be that these days we tend to think of our landscapes in terms of needs rather than beliefs. After all, it's a generally acknowledged fact that our landscapes must be environmentally designed to aid in our survival. But we also experience great joy when we encounter landscapes that formally display the environmental ideal—a green roof, for example, or a reconstructed headland.

This is not to say that a mingling of need and belief mandates any one design form. Indeed, far from it! We must rely on designers who are able to objectify that cultural web in the designed landscapes that surround us. These designers rely on consultants to make those environmental landscapes actually work, and when things go right they also gain a wider benefit, one that goes beyond the functional. Consultants influence the designer with a specialized knowledge that, far from leading to one formal solution, extends the possibilities of form. As Walker emphasizes: "Technicians bring things together and add to your awareness of opportunities, to your ability to be more precise, more elegant, more daring. Their knowledge expands your possibilities. They enable the designer to go beyond craft. They enable the designer to build a wider range of ideas."

top: Barangaroo construction site – left to right: Jay Swaintek, Kieron Little, and Troy Stratti

middle: Stuart Pittendrigh and Simon Leake at Barangaroo Reserve, 2014

bottom: Barangaroo construction site – left to right: Barry Murphy, Peter Walker, Mizuki Stratti, and Troy Stratti

PROJECTS

Beginning in the mid-nineteenth century a long portion of the foreshore of Sydney Harbour was filled in to create space for maritime industrialization, a practice continuing a century later when the New South Wales Maritime Services Board replaced some aging wooden wharves with a container port constructed of concrete. From 2009 to 2015 PWP worked on a project that opened up some of the last available waterfront footage to development. Lying directly west of the Central Business District and The Rocks (Sydney's oldest neighborhood), Barangaroo is made up of three areas: Barangaroo South, a 7.5-hectare mix of office and residential development; Barangaroo Central, a 5.7-hectare mixed-use/open space; and Barangaroo Reserve, a 6-hectare re-creation of a historic headland on the site of the old container port. Barangaroo Reserve completes the northern face of Sydney, a stunning landscape of points including Mrs. Macquarie's Chair at the Royal Botanic Gardens, Bennalong Point and the Sydney Opera House, Dawes Point and the Sydney Harbour Bridge. Barangaroo

Barangaroo
Reserve

Sydney, Australia

**PLAN OF SYDNEY
HARBOUR WALK**

━━━ Existing Sydney shoreline
public right-of-way

▬▬▬ Right-of-way blocked by
container port

also restores the visual and symbolic geography of the islands and headlands that were home to the indigenous people of the Eora Nation at the time of European arrival.

The landscape architects' guidelines define the design vocabulary for the entire public domain as well as its connections to Sydney's Central Business District and several adjacent historic neighborhoods, including such concerns as paving, furniture, lighting, plant palettes, way-finding, and seawall and promenade design. This shared vocabulary serves to unite three areas with very different programs. Pedestrian routes, dedicated bicycle paths, a new ferry terminal, and a new metro station will increase accessibility between the areas and to other parts of the city. At the edge of Sydney

Harbour, Wulugul Walk—developed with a unified vocabulary of sandstone, timber boardwalks, site furniture, and tree canopies—will complete the 14-kilometer Sydney Harbour Walk, an uninterrupted path from Woolloomooloo to the Anzac Bridge passing by such landmarks as the Botanic Garden, the Opera House, the Harbour Bridge, Walsh Bay, Darling Harbour, and the ANZAC and Iron Cove bridges.

Barangaroo South is a mixed-use precinct with commercial office buildings, retail offerings, residential apartments, an international hotel, a Crown casino, restaurants, and cultural facilities. It positions Sydney as a key financial center in the Asian Pacific, with 23,000 new jobs predicted as a result of the development. Entrances at Hickson Road,

top: Sydney container port circa 1960

bottom: Rendering of Barangaroo North, Central, and South upon completion

two bridges, and a new underground pedestrian link from the Wynward train station will connect Barangaroo South to the Central Business District. A new ferry terminal will offset the high concentration at Circular Quay. One of PWP's most challenging political tasks, to date, has been overseeing the design of Barangaroo South to ensure continuity of the public domain design vocabulary and the public right-of-way of Wulugul Walk.

Central Barangaroo, which connects the historic Millers Point neighborhood to the water, is half mixed-use development and cultural buildings, half open space, including a large turf area for programmed festivals and entertainment. A grove of canopy trees creates a civic space at the Hickson Road entrance,

and the tree-lined Wulugul Walk passes along the newly excavated Nawi Cove to join Central with South Barangaroo and Barangaroo Reserve. Slabs of sandstone arranged like shingles gently slope through the tidal zone and transition into broad seat-high steps. The proposed Sydney Steps will tie the Central Business District to both Central and South Barangaroo.

At Barangaroo Reserve a Club Cape headland was re-created by a close collaboration of specialists working with PWP: stone mason Troy Stratti, soils scientist and engineer Simon Leake, and horticulturalist Stuart Pittendrigh. PWP was guided initially by geomorphologic studies as well as hand-drawn historical maps and such early depictions as Major Taylor's three panoramic views of

LANDSCAPE MASTER PLAN
OF PRECINCT

1   Millers Point
2   Barangaroo Point
3   Moores Wharf
4   Towns Place Entrance
5   Argyle Place Entrance
6   Hickson Entrance
7   Nawi Cove
8   Public Foreshore Promenade –
    Wulugul Walk
9   Upper Bluff – Stargazer Lawn
10 Burrawang Steps
11 Baludarri Steps
12 Girra Girra Steps
13 Lift
14 Waranara Terrace –
    Cutaway Cultural Space Entrance
15 Bush Terrace Café
16 Bush Land and Bush Walk
17 Historic Seawall
18 Dukes Pier
19 Historic Munns Slipway
20 Historic Cuthberts Seawall
21 Sydney Steps
22 Sailors Return Park
23 Barangaroo Promenade
24 Hickson Park
25 Watermans Cove
26 Barangaroo Ferry Hub
27 Exchange Place
28 Wynyard Walk

FORM

Before the European arrival the Aboriginals lived on a circle of five headlands surrounding what is now known as Goat Island. The land was connected by small boats. The inhabitants were fishermen and modest farmers. No records of the morphology, size, and shape of the destroyed headland exist except for paintings and drawings.

Physical and computer models explored these drawings to determine the form of the new headland.

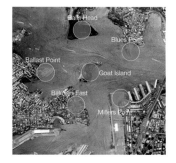

Five headlands surrounding
Goat Island

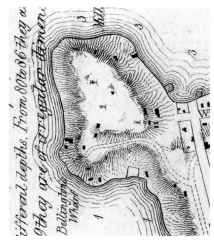

Historic drawing of Barangaroo

PLANTING

Research of both existing urbanized and natural headlands informed the proposed planting, which is based on plants native to Sydney and includes historic variations that would have been present on the western and southern slopes. From the outside the planting appears solid. From inside it allows framed views of the harbor.

The proposed plants were grown in a nursery north of Sydney in soil manufactured from the site excavations. They were then carefully transported to the site and replanted in the same manufactured soil.

Existing headland

STONE

At the base of the existing headlands the water's edge is protected by a beach made of stones that over time have fallen and then been eroded by wave action. This became the model for the water's edge at Barangaroo.

All rainwater runoff is captured and stored in underground cisterns, then recycled for irrigation.

Fallen stone beach at existing headland

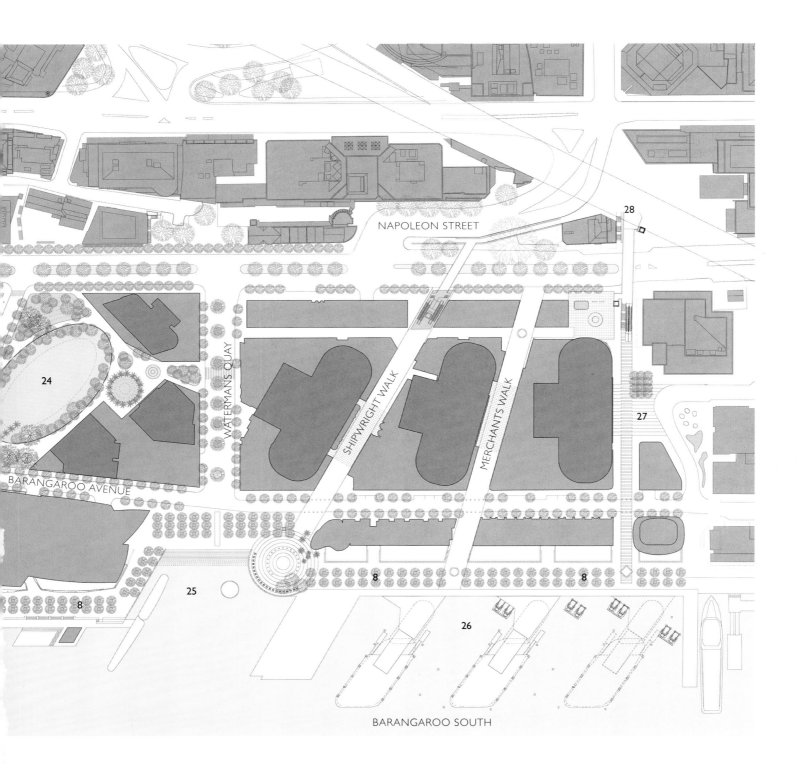

NAPOLEON STREET

WATERMANS QUAY

SHIPWRIGHT WALK

MERCHANTS WALK

BARANGAROO AVENUE

28

24

27

8

25

8

8

26

BARANGAROO SOUTH

left: Hickson Road entry
to Barangaroo Reserve

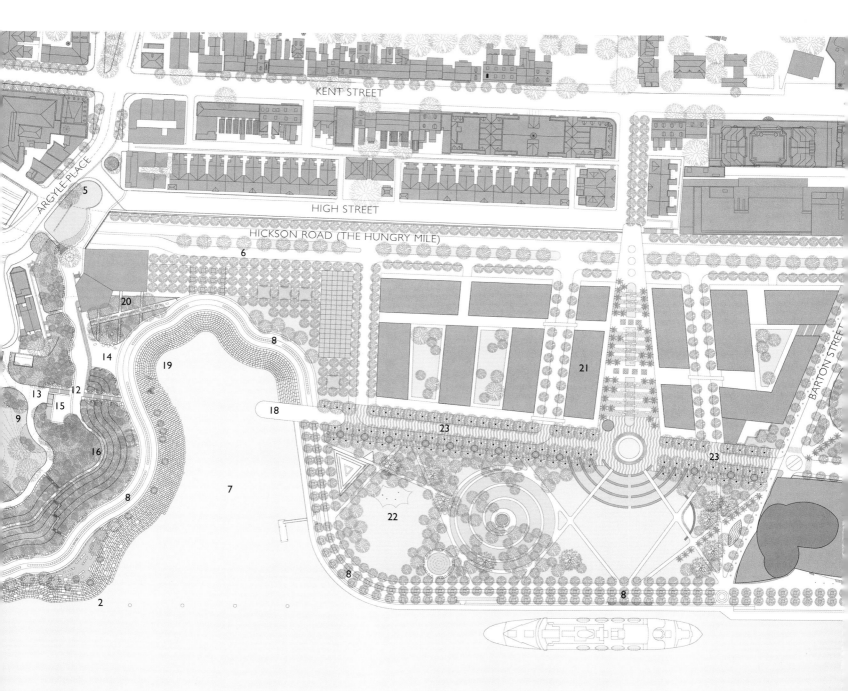

KENT STREET

ARGYLE PLACE

5

HIGH STREET

HICKSON ROAD (THE HUNGRY MILE)

6

20

14

19

8

13

12

15

9

16

8

18

23

21

7

22

23

2

8

8

CENTRAL BARANGAROO

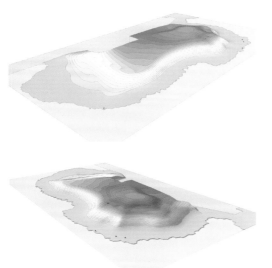

Computer models

Historic painting of the headland
at time of European arrival

A water view from inside
the headland bush

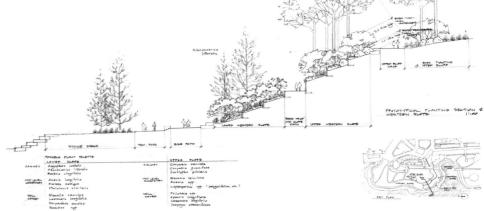

Typical proposed planting plan
with historic species

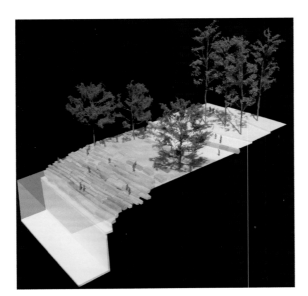

Model of naturalistic reconstructed
stone shoreline

top: Stratti rocksaw
bottom: On-site sandstone quarry

First mock-up of foreshore stones

Projected profile of new headland

Projected form of new headland park

*75,000 new plants,
all native to Sydney*

Stones taken from quarry

*Placement of stones with newly
designed handling equipment*

*Naturalistic stone beach placed
at water's edge*

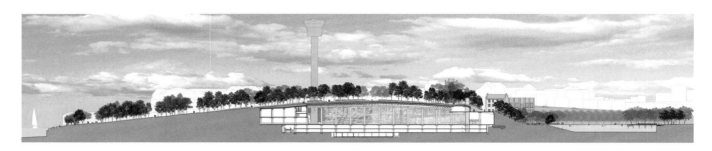

*top: Section showing event space
and parking garage beneath the
reconstructed headland*

*bottom: Foreshore boardwalk
Central Barangaroo*

Sydney (1817-1822). Stratti, chief stone mason for Balderstone, was in charge of the quarry operation, creating the foreshore with the artful installation of 10,000 large sandstone blocks—the foundation of Sydney Harbour—excavated from the middle of the site. The complicated design required a customized software modeling program and GPS technology, setting a new global benchmark for naturalistic construction; cut from the ancient rock, each block was barcoded and tracked using a smartphone app. The materials removed from the existing site during the quarry operations and the reshaping

of the container port and Nawi Cove were ground up for base-fill layers and creation of the headland. Leake developed strategies to produce a blended soil from the crushed and washed stone waste that maximized the growth of Pittendrigh's bush planting scheme. These plantings are native, not just to Australia but specifically to the Sydney area; they were pregrown at Andreasens Green Nursery at Mangrove Mountain, two hours north of Sydney, with Pittendrigh supervising the pregrowing and installation. After two years the pregrown bush plants had reached a substantial size at installation.

Pedestrian and bicycle pathways wind along the headland, separated by a low one-meter-wide sandstone wall that is a symbolic marker of the original pre-colonial shoreline, the rusticated stone masonry of the "1836 Wall" evoking the first colonial sandstone constructions of Sydney. An accessible main walk-way moves gently up the north slope from Wulugul Walk, terminating at the Stargazer Lawn, the highest point of the headland, which is shaded by large Morton Bay fig trees and eucalyptus. Bush planting discretely conceals the elevator that serves the underground spaces created by the excavation of

top: View from top of headland

bottom: View from shoreline to top of headland

*above: Native tropical planting
on steep southern slope*

the sandstone blocks: a 300-car public garage and the Cutaway, a large room—50 by 150 meters—that recalls indigenous cave dwellings and is intended to serve as a cultural center.

Ecological methods were key in restoring this huge expanse of empty concrete container port into humane, naturalistic, usable space. The most complex ecological system is the bush, which consists of three planting layers: 1) a ground-plane of plants such as *Lomandra longifolia* (mat rush) and *Hardenbergia violacea* (native sarsaparilla), which are about one-half meter to two meters in height; 2) an understory of plants such as *Acacia longifolia* (Sydney golden wattle), which are up to approximately five meters in height and give Barangaroo the distinctive shape of existing Sydney headlands; and 3) a canopy of trees such as *Angophora costata* (smooth bark apple), *Eucalyptus pilularis* (blackbutt), and *Eucalyptus saligna* (Sydney blue gum), which are 10 to 20 meters in height and create a series of cathedral-like spaces above the bush planting layers. The plant palette in the northern and western portion of the bush facing Sydney Harbour and with more sun exposure differs from the more shaded and temperate portion facing south.

In order to achieve the goal of becoming the first precinct of its size in the world to be climate positive, all three districts of Barangaroo have followed sustainable principles in the planning and design process. Barangaroo has been selected as one of 17 major developments worldwide to participate in the Clinton Climate Initiative Development Program, which supports large-scale urban projects that reduce on-site CO_2 emissions to zero. The project exemplifies the ten One Planet Living principles, which provide the guidelines for sustainable development: Zero Carbon, Zero Waste, Sustainable Transport, Sustainable Materials, Local and Sustainable Foods, Sustainable Water, Land Use and Wildlife, Cultural and Community, Equity and Local Economy, and Health and Happiness. For example, using the 10,000 blocks of sandstone excavated from the site to construct the foreshore edge eliminated the transport of thousands of truck-loads of materials through the city. Other materials were locally sourced, and the nearly 10,000 native plants were pregrown locally. The foreshore was designed to promote habitat for marine life and fish, and the park has been an immediate attraction for several important bird species. Electrical demands will be satisfied by solar panels incorporated into the vast range of Barangaroo South buildings.

top: Vines on stone retaining walls

bottom: Planting at water's edge

Equally important was telling people about the project. Construction initiatives included a continuous program of public outreach and involvement with movies and articles, the employment of indigenous people, a series of public "open days," New Year's Eve celebrations, and programmed cultural events.

One of the foremost purposes for reconstructing the headland was to reestablish the symbolic geography that reminds us of Sydney's long pre-European indigenous past. No one has been more vocal in explaining Barangaroo's role in this regard than former Prime Minister Paul Keating. At the time of European settlement Goat Island was occupied and owned by Bennelong and his wife, Barangaroo. The island, which they appropriately called Memel (a local word for "the eye"), lay at the center of a concentric ring of other Aboriginal

locales including what we now call Ballast Point, Balls Head, McMahons Point, Millers Point, and the eastern tip of Balmain. The physical re-creation offered by Barangaroo Reserve fulfills a goal adopted in 2005 by the Sydney Harbour Foreshore Authority as part of a larger plan to showcase Aboriginal culture.

Barangaroo Reserve also acknowledges the culture that took root after the Europeans arrived. Early photographs indicate that neighborhoods adjacent to the headland at Millers Point had fine-grained streets and lanes and many examples of colonial buildings that were demolished to make room for industrialization in the 1920s. Towns Place, for example, was a bustling waterfront with many buildings, and Argyle Place was surrounded by colonial structures. Towns Place now functions as the main entrance to Barangaroo Reserve with

top: View over pedestrian and bicycle paths to foreshore and Sydney Harbour from bush planted six months earlier

facing page: Activities on opening days

Phase II
top: Foreshore pathway along
proposed Green Park

bottom: Proposed Green Park at
Central Barangaroo looking north

facing page:
top left: Proposed outdoor digital
theater and path to Hickson Park

bottom left: Proposed pedestrian
street joining the headland with
southern commercial and retail center

top right: Proposed Sydney Steps
amphitheater

bottom right: Proposed raised stage
at base of Sydney Steps

access to the underground parking area, while Argyle Place has been developed as a revitalized town square. The new plan, developed jointly with the City, widens pedestrian zones, reduces asphalt, and provides trees, furniture, and amenities so that people can walk and gather comfortably.

Barangaroo Reserve unites its concern for natural processes with cultural references. For example, the sandstone so abundantly used in the project makes a historical reference to old Sydney, which developed on top of the stone and hence used it extensively as building material. Another example was the naming process conducted by the Barangaroo Delivery Authority, working closely with such key stakeholders as the City of Sydney, the Metropolitan Local Aboriginal Land Council, the La Perouse Local

Aboriginal Land Council, Lend Lease, and the New South Wales Geographical Names Board. Names reflect Aboriginal culture, prominent Sydneysiders, and the history of the local area, themes that were also popular in the 2006 public competition that produced the name "Barangaroo." The Authority's approach has been to ensure that names for the northern area of Barangaroo reference Aboriginal people and culture, with names for other parts of the precinct evenly distributed across historical, natural, nautical, and urban themes. The following are a few examples:

- Nawi Cove is named for a type of Aboriginal canoe; similarly Wulugul Walk is named for a type of fish, the Walumil Steps for the Port Jackson shark, and the Girra Girra Steps for seagulls;

- Watermans Cove recalls a historical form of employment for nineteenth-century residents, as do names for Watermans Quay, Shipwright Walk, and Merchants Walk;

- and Scotch Row, a pedestrian walk at Barangaroo South, takes its name from the area that housed master stonemasons brought out from Scotland to Sydney, where local works include the Lord Nelson Hotel, a favorite after-work site for PWP staff.

top: Stone entry gate from Towns Place

bottom: Children playing on future stone fountain

next page: Event space with retained sandstone cliff wall

University of Texas at Dallas

Dallas, Texas

Existing campus character, 2006:

Library Square

Central campus

Square at Student Center

Entry road through
athletic fields

The 485-acre University of Texas at Dallas was originally developed in the 1960s by Texas Instruments cofounders Eugene McDermott, Cecil Green, and J. Eric Jonsson as a training school for their employees. It was given to the State of Texas in 1969 and, over the years, lost the natural landscape and creek corridors that historically graced the property, leaving it a collection of Brutalist buildings set within a sea of asphalt parking lots and expansive paved pedestrian pathways. In 2006 PWP began work on a Campus Site Development Master Plan for expansion through the year 2050. The goals of the master plan include a commitment to landscape-led development and site planning, a pedestrian-based hierarchy of circulation, the creation of microclimates and landscaped paths for walking and biking within the campus, and a long-range parking-garage strategy to transition away from expansive surface parking. Most significantly, the master plan calls for the creation of new outdoor spaces to transform the public realm of the overall campus environment. These spaces would play a critical role in providing informal and organized social activities for students; places for spontaneous interaction between faculty, students, and visitors; and areas for outdoor study, meetings, and public events.

The master plan provides a strategy that sequences improvements for the public realm as the campus continues to expand and rebuild many of its outdated buildings. Design for Phase One of the University of Texas at Dallas Campus Landscape Enhancement Project was initiated in 2007 with construction beginning in January 2009. The first phase of work, a gift from Margaret McDermott and her late husband, was designed to integrate the existing buildings and grounds of different eras and disparate design into a beautiful campus entrance and central mall while still allowing for future growth. Key components of the design included a formal southern campus entry, an entry drive, a contemporary version of the traditional campus quad, and a central plaza at the core of the campus.

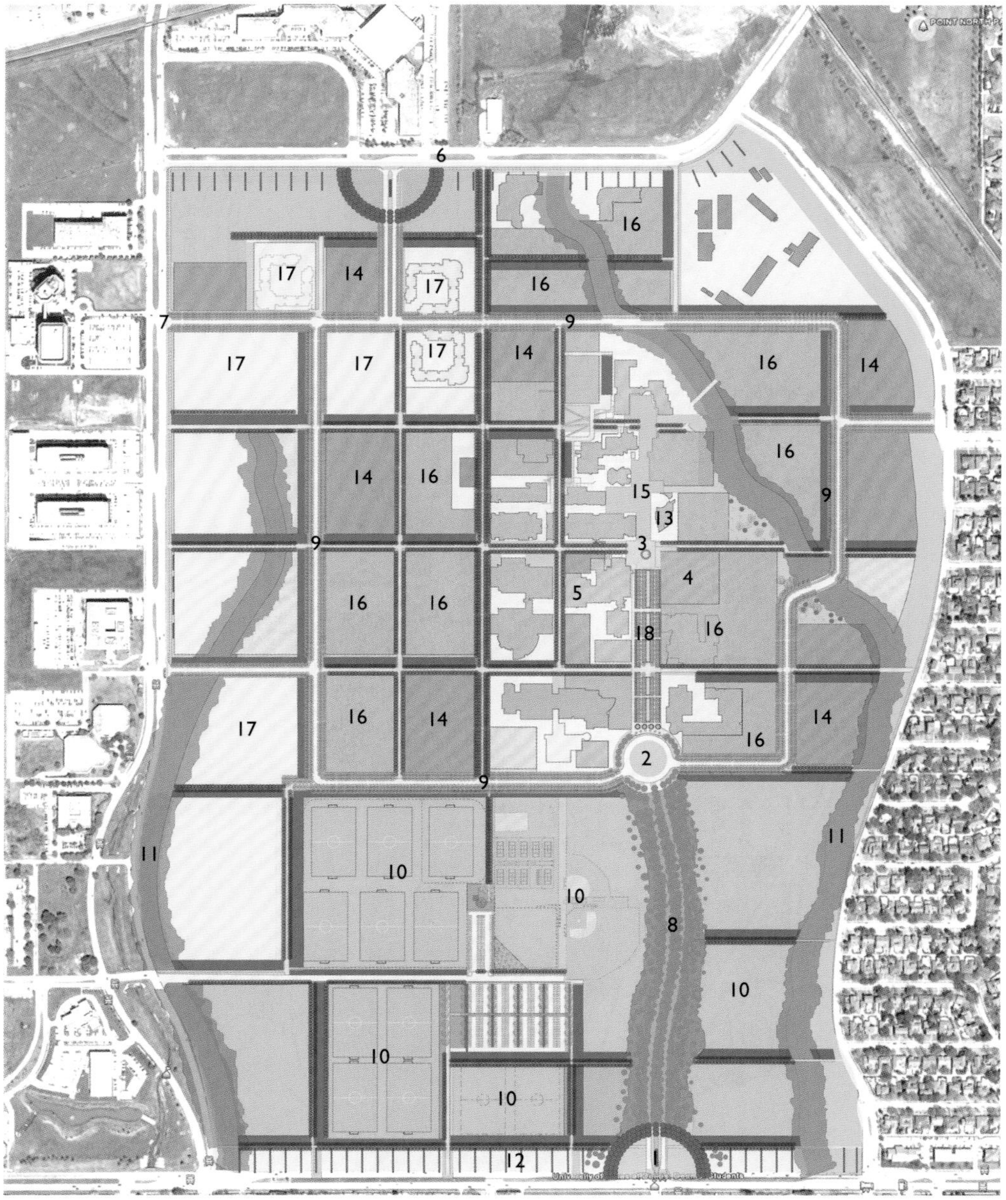

CAMPUS MASTER PLAN

1 Main Entry
2 Arrival Court
3 Central Plaza
4 Library
5 Student Union
6 North Entry
7 West Entry
8 Entrance Grove
9 Loop Road
10 Recreation
11 Restored Creek
12 Hedge Garden
13 Green Theater
14 Parking
15 North Mall
16 Academic Expansion
17 Housing
18 South Mall

top: Magnolia-lined Mall with reflecting pools

bottom: Entry road with new "creek-side" planting

The new southern entrance to the campus was created with 33 matched hedges of native hollies, each 120 feet long, planted in a meadow of tall grasses along the 3,200 linear feet of campus frontage on Campbell Road. A large crescent of transplanted live oaks and a monumental campus entrance sign initiate the 1.1-mile-long University Parkway, which embraces a newly restored creek and has been planted with more than two acres of native woodland habitat including some 5,000 trees. It will develop into a natural forest with wildflowers and meadow grasses requiring little or no maintenance. Curb-cuts placed along the drive's median direct stormwater into the new woodland habitat, now recognized as one of the largest rain gardens in the Dallas region. A new bike path connects Campbell Road to the central core of the campus through the forest of trees.

University Parkway ends at a large mounded sculptural traffic circle that transitions to the Mall and ties into the new vehicular Loop Road around the perimeter of the campus. The Mall is almost 1,000 feet long and defined by a series of five rectilinear pools flanked by stately lines of columnar magnolias and walkways. Each pool is outlined by low cut-sandstone walls and interrupted by hundreds of bubblers that gently break the surface of the pools with patterns that look like raindrops. A new Student Services Building and Edith O'Donnell Arts and Technology Building have been constructed along with the Mall.

The Mall transitions to Central Plaza, which connects the existing Student Union and the Eugene McDermott Library. It is defined by a one-acre 26-foot-high trellis of recycled steel and fiber-reinforced plastic partially covered by wisteria vines; it provides filtered shade and helps reflect heat. At the center of the plaza, a simple circular pool incorporates a stainless steel column with a fog system from which a mist rises above the trellis to cool the space. At the side of this venue a stepped seating area (made of recycled ipe wood)

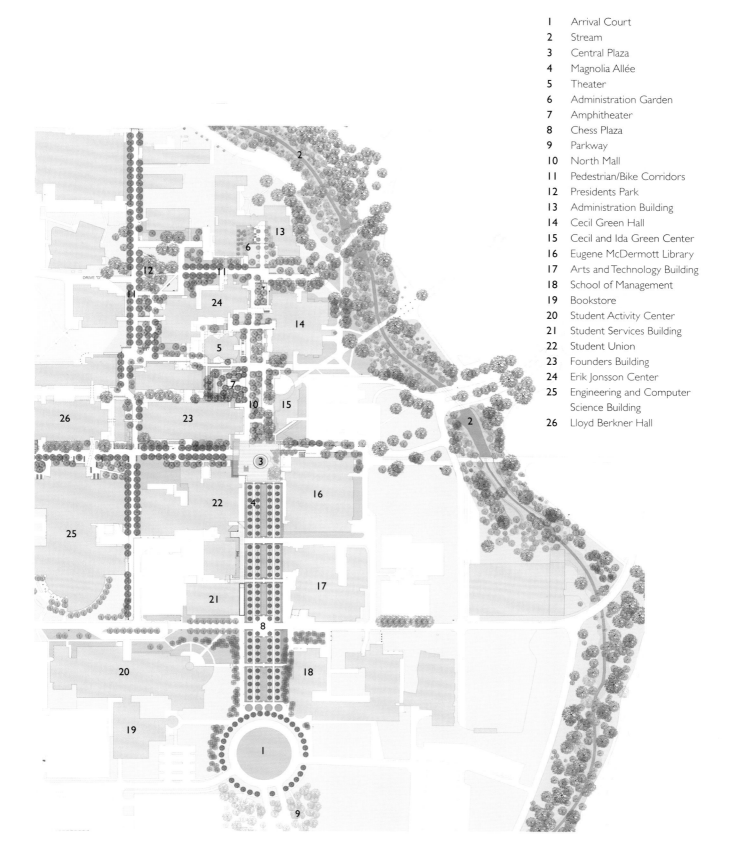

1   Arrival Court
2   Stream
3   Central Plaza
4   Magnolia Allée
5   Theater
6   Administration Garden
7   Amphitheater
8   Chess Plaza
9   Parkway
10   North Mall
11   Pedestrian/Bike Corridors
12   Presidents Park
13   Administration Building
14   Cecil Green Hall
15   Cecil and Ida Green Center
16   Eugene McDermott Library
17   Arts and Technology Building
18   School of Management
19   Bookstore
20   Student Activity Center
21   Student Services Building
22   Student Union
23   Founders Building
24   Erik Jonsson Center
25   Engineering and Computer
      Science Building
26   Lloyd Berkner Hall

97

top left: Chess tournament on the Mall

top right: Chess practice

bottom: Students at Central Plaza

facing page: Aerial view of Central Plaza and the Mall

provides a convenient place for student and faculty interaction. Two digital-clock walls reference the campus's origins with Texas Instruments. As a tribute to the university's nationally ranked chess team, a Chess Plaza located at a central point in the Mall incorporates four large chess boards designed into the paving. The Mall and the Central Plaza have become regular settings for major campus events and gatherings.

Many of the materials for the project were locally sourced and are well-suited to a long life span; 97 percent of the plant material is native and requires minimal irrigation and maintenance; the Mall is drained by perforated pipe, allowing infiltration of stormwater into the water table; 33 acres of land have been reforested; and, most important, the design has removed an existing concrete drainage channel and implemented a forest-creek restoration that filters and infiltrates stormwater. The overall design reduces impervious surfaces by 49 percent, 4.3 acres in the Mall.

The new landscape creates spaces for student activity and, equally important, a visual identity that can engender campus pride, aid in the recruitment of students and new funding, and provide a civic amenity for the surrounding suburbs. Since the opening of the new landscape in 2010, the public image of the campus has been transformed. In a recent survey

- 87 percent of campus users including students, faculty, and staff said it improved their perception of the campus and the university;
- 44 percent of the students surveyed stated that it influenced their decision to apply and enroll;
- and 70 percent of campus users said it improved the quality of life, primarily reducing stress and providing better spaces to be outdoors and meet friends.

The project has stimulated university fundraising, and since the completion of the Phase One Campus Enhancements, student enrollment has grown by more than 30 percent.

100

PHASE TWO

The second phase was also supported by a generous gift from Margaret Mc-Dermott. In June 2012 PWP updated the previous campus landscape master plan, which now creates a new development framework including guidelines for

- definition of the campus public realm through landscape;
- placement of new buildings;
- an integrated campus circulation system for pedestrians, bicycles, cars, emergency vehicles, and buses;
- parking;
- water management;
- open space and recreation facilities;
- and creek restoration.

The key components of Phase Two focus on an extension of the Mall north to the Administration Building; complete reconstruction of major pedestrian paths; new pedestrian and bicycle paths

that respond to the influence of the new student residential complex at the north end of the campus; and new public spaces for gatherings, study, and events. Design commenced on a phased implementation strategy in August 2012.

The northern extension of the Mall creates a series of shaded landscape paths and outdoor gathering spaces; overall the new construction reduces the paved and impervious surfaces by 60 percent. A significant new public outdoor area was created along the Mall incorporating a series of stone and grass terraces encompassing three sides of a small plaza space and fountain. Trees were designed into the terraces providing welcome shade and comfort. Throughout the remainder of the Mall, extensive seating areas have been provided through sandstone benches, picnic tables, and moveable tables and chairs. New lighting has been incorporated throughout to extend use into the evening.

top: Wooden amphitheater

bottom: Students at the Mall

The pedestrian path extending west from the Central Plaza to Rutford Avenue has been redesigned to accommodate pedestrians, bicycles, and emergency vehicles. Additionally, a new north-south pedestrian-and-bike path has been created to link the northern edge of campus to the Student Activity Center on the south. The paths have been generously planted with cedar elms and live oaks. Seating areas, bike parking, and new public gathering spaces are provided throughout the corridors. All paths have been lighted and designed to be ADA-accessible.

PWP designed a new trellis over the west pedestrian path along the Phase One Mall linking the Student Services Building to the Student Union. This now completes a weather-protected linkage along the west portion of the Mall. With the completion of the Phase Two landscape improvements more than 70 acres of the campus public realm have been transformed.

top: Grass and stone amphitheater

bottom: Pedestrian path to Administration Building

Sydney Olympic Park

Sydney, Australia

View of the Parramatta River from the site, 2015

In 1997 the Olympic Coordination Authority selected a team led by HASSELL, an architecture, urban design, and landscape architecture firm in Sydney, to create the concept plan for a 1,600-acre park surrounding the main site of the 2000 Sydney Olympic Games at Homebush Bay. The role of PWP was to provide leadership in the formulation of the design concept for the site. PWP drew upon Tony McCormick of HASSELL and Bruce Mackenzie of Bruce Mackenzie Design for local knowledge and specific skills. McCormick also included specialists on the team to inform the design of a project that demanded a merger of artistic ingenuity, scientific knowledge, and construction skill. The success of the project depended on the skills of experts in the fields of ecology, nature conservation, hydraulic and civil engineering, lighting and solar energy, and geotechnics and soil.

The role of the design team was to realize the key objective of the original bid for the games: restoration of the vast surrounding landscape, which was one of the most polluted industrial sites in the world. One of the greatest challenges was that grading had already begun by the time the designers arrived on the scene, and, put on the same schedule, with only a few years before the games, they were challenged to stay ahead of various associated site-development schedules. In addition, other design teams were responsible for parallel projects such as the urban core of the Homebush Bay Olympic Games site, Athletes Village, and individual sports venues.

Australian landscape architect Catherin Bull has pointed out the pervasive influence of the eighteenth-century Picturesque in the design of Australian parks, what she calls "a unique form of imperialism." Sydney Olympic Park would, in part, be created as a contrast to this Picturesque ideal with a visual character that more honestly expressed Australia's aspirations for and relationship to the land in the twenty-first century. Once the home of the Wann-gal Aboriginal people, the site was nearly twice as large as New York City's Central Park. Unlike Central Park, it did not lie within an urban grid and had no formal boundaries. Rather, it had been cobbled together out of various governmental parcels, most of which had suffered ecological degradation by various industrial uses in the nineteenth and twentieth centuries. These included abattoirs, meat-and-hide-processing industries, military uses, quarrying, and

PARAMATTA
RIVER

LANDSCAPE
PLAN OF PARK

1   Haslams Creek
2   Brick Pit
3   Central Parking
4   Bicentennial Park
5   Refurbished Mangrove
6   Munitions Base
7   Marker

Olympic Center

Lawn / Meadow

Reclaimed Water

Reforestation

--- Paths

108

above: *Proposed revitalized industrial waterfront on the Parramatta River*

chemical- and heavy-manufacturing facilities. More than 65 percent of the site was contaminated to some degree with chemical waste, which had to be excavated, treated, and capped before the site could be used for recreational purposes. The site's main waterway, Haslams Creek, had been filled with contaminated material that supported neither flora nor fauna and destroyed its natural flow. Specific legislation dictated that these toxic materials could not be removed from the site. Additionally, a portion of the site had been a naval arsenal and arms-reprocessing center during the nineteenth century, World War I, and World War II. Unexploded munitions had been buried under-ground and were still present along the filled creek.

Nevertheless, the site possessed remarkable assets: more than 12 kilometers of continuous waterfront along Haslams Creek, the Parramatta River, and Homebush Bay; a number of historic buildings from the military base dating back more than a century; a rare and unspoiled 119-acre remnant forest; substantial areas of mangrove swamp

in the major inlets and river edge, some of which had been developed and maintained for habitat conservation; bird sanctuaries in the mangrove stands; and endangered Golden Orb spiders and Green and Golden Bell frogs.

Working with information provided by an ongoing team of environmental consultants, PWP created a concept plan with three unifying design themes: lowlands (functioning waterways and wetlands); "walls and rooms" (green corridors separating various ecosystems and activity areas); and elevated land-forms. Bruce Mackenzie, a proponent of "Sydney Bush design," created a unifying site-wide planting strategy.

In the design scheme Haslams Creek was restored into a naturalistic stream-bed leading down to the Parramatta River; a series of freshwater wetlands harvested urban runoff for irrigation use and naturally purified the water before discharge into the river; and the surrounding area was replanted as a major riparian wetland with a variety of grasses, reeds, and aquatic plants.

108

Extensive reforestation with native trees formed a series of continuous "walls" around each parkland "room," thus putting each recreational function into its own identifiable setting or "place." Parcels were connected by a system of paths within the "walls"—shaded green tubes for walking, bicycling, and jogging. Existing automobile boulevards were replanted. Access was restricted in ecologically sensitive areas such as the forest and salt marshes as well as the culturally significant former naval armaments base.

Since the contaminated soil and excess fill from the sports precinct construction could not be moved off-site, it was placed in landforms including naturalistic hills and ziggurats, 20 to 60 meters high, which serve as orientation posts at the five entrances. Tree planting was kept to the deeper soil at the lower edges on the landforms, while the thin caps were sown with native grasses. Spiraling paths lead to the tops of the markers and views of the Olympic stadia, the park, and the Sydney skyline in the distance.

The prairie-like grassland and historic buildings of the former naval base (and its munitions storehouses) were retained along with the 119-acre forest area. The former small-gauge railway, which had been used to transport missiles and torpedoes around the military site, is now a ride for visitors. In Bicentennial Park—a major parcel within the parklands—mangrove swamps were reestablished, thereby doubling bird and insect habitat. An aerial walkway provides an education venue for the 70-acre Brick Pit, an old sandstone and clay quarry that serves as both a habitat for the endangered frogs and a historical monument (a source of the sandstone and bricks from which Sydney was built). A continuous boardwalk and bicycle promenade stretches the full length of the frontage on the Parramatta River, incorporating historic wharves, a new restaurant, and a ferry terminal into the new visitor experience.

top: Proposed replanted wetlands at Haslams Creek

bottom: Proposed marker at major park entries

Armament depot

The Brick Pit

Degraded site from the air

Green and Golden Bell frog, an endangered species living in the Brick Pit

Boardwalk through the mangrove swamp

Munitions vault

Brick manufacturing

Munitions storage

*Working wharf along the
Parramatta River*

*Underground storage
for ammunition*

Victorian train station

Remnant Victorian buildings

Existing service railroad

When reclamation began the land would support neither flora nor fauna. None of this contaminated soil could be legally exported from the site. Some existing elements could be retained in the new park. At the time the park was being designed grading was already under way.

New water-reclamation pond

Grading done before design

Rebuilding waterways

EXTRACTION AND FILL

Excavation

Fill

Marker over contaminated soil

New earthen hills with grassed cap above
damaged soil and trees planted in alluvial
soil at the base

Establishment of wetlands along
reclaimed Haslams Creek

Ziggurat-marker form over contaminated soil

top: Viewing structure within preserved Brick Pit (Durlach Block Jaggers, architect), 2005

middle left: View from top of marker

right: Bicycle rally on new grass field

bottom left: Picnic in the shade of planted trees

right: Performance tent

Throughout the site remediation, which—thanks to Simon Leake—included the world's first large-scale use of facsimile soils, decontamination activities were not hidden in traditional scenic treatments but celebrated both physically (the ziggurat-markers of excess fill, for example) and through interpretation. In this way the park, as Catherin Bull points out, "takes its own development as a central theme in its program, thus becoming one of the first self-referential parks in the world." The Sydney Olympic Park Authority was subsequently established to manage the development of the park and its evolving program. Not unlike a small university, it blends the study of cultural and natural history with site-specific arts, scholars and artists in residence, education and outreach programs, and recreational facilities as well as exhibitions, festivals, and commemorations, thereby expanding the commercial activities of the urban core and events like the annual Easter Show throughout the year.

Fifteen years later, on any given week-end, the park is filled with bicyclers, hikers, soccer players, and archers as well as families enjoying picnics and birthday parties. Development pressure increases as new apartment blocks and commercial buildings vie for position at the park boundaries. The visual character of the park has been successfully established by its now-mature plantings and natural areas, but the ultimate value of the park is not limited to its design. We can all enjoy and learn from its exemplary story of Before and After.

above: Homebush Bay Ferry Terminal (Alexander Tzannes & Associates, architect), 1997

right: Armory Wharf Cafe at river's edge (Lahz Minno, architect), 2008

top left: New playground and bike path to river's edge (James Mather Delaney Design, landscape architect), 2005

top right: Bike path through planted casuarina and eucalyptus forest, 2005

facing page: Aerial view of 1,500-acre park with the Olympic Center at lower right and surrounding new private development

bottom left: Natural grassed hillside mound

bottom right: Reforestation to form green "rooms"

*Casuarina and eucalyptus forest
with native grass understory*

top: Wooden pathway through
replanted marshland at
Haslams Creek

bottom: Pathway through
replanted native grasslands

"Finite, Infinite"

Beijing, China

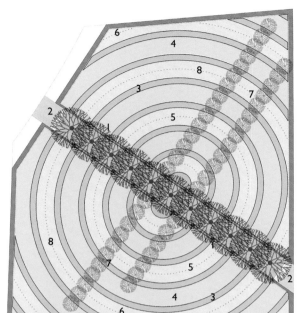

LANDSCAPE PLAN

1 Mirror Walls
2 Plane Trees in Cobble Field
3 Boxwood Hedges
4 Grass
5 Gravel
6 Wood Bench
7 Poplar Allée
8 Flush Lights

In 2013 the Beijing International Garden Exposition invited internationally respected landscape architects to design eight separate gardens to be the centerpiece of EXPO 2013. PWP joint-ventured their garden with BAM (Ballistic Architecture Machine), a young landscape-design firm located in Beijing, whose partners—Jacob Schwartz Walker, Daniel Gass, and Allison Dailey—have been practicing in China since 2009.

"Finite, Infinite" is made up of two parallel double-sided mirrors 176 feet long and 12 feet high, placed 16 feet from each other. Between the inside mirrors, 11 sycamores are planted 17 feet from each other. This arrangement creates a "barber-shop" effect that stretches the viewed row of trees into an infinite orchard of exactly matching trees growing out of a rough cobble floor. To increase the geometric drama, white-wash bands are painted on the tree trunks. Above, 18 strings of small lights strung from mirror wall to mirror wall seemingly stretch to infinity.

On both sides of the outside mirrors, a series of concentric half-circles of boxwood hedges and gravel produce (thanks to the mirrors) finite completed circles in two identical parterre embroideries. Carved stone steps on either side of the mirrored tunnel are drilled with holes that light the risers. The stone adds a note of antiquity to the composition by its contrast to the refined mirror walls. Around the perimeter of the garden an elegant bench made of fitted wooden slats accommodates visitors.

The whole garden is exquisitely crafted, thanks to BAM's detailed construction drawings and on-site supervision, something rarely achieved in contemporary Chinese gardens.

*top: Half-circular parterre
completed by mirror*

*bottom: Double row of
poplars marching through
circular hedges extended
into mirror*

Infinite orchard of striped trees

top: Mirrors with a single row
of plane trees

bottom: Mirrors extending lights

*Stone steps leading
into the mirrored infinity hall*

Glenstone

Potomac, Maryland

Replanted flowering meadow

Located on more than 200 acres in Potomac, Maryland, Glenstone is a place that integrates art, architecture, and landscape. For more than a decade PWP has been working to develop this property—once slated to be a residential subdivision—into an ideal setting for quiet aesthetic contemplation. Here visitors can form meaningful connections with some of the past century's most significant works of art in an environmentally sensitive landscape that incorporates outdoor sculpture, rolling topography, native meadows, a restored stream and pond, and a web of pedestrian pathways.

PHASE ONE

When first acquired by its present owner, the Glenstone property was structured as a series of small plateaus separated by slopes, discreet one-to-five-acre plots graded to receive single-family houses. The project's initial goal was to reshape this subdivided land and integrate it with the surrounding topography of the Potomac River Valley while simultaneously creating an ecologically sustainable strategy of landscape management. The ultimate objective was the creation of a series of outdoor spaces where both architecture and sculpture could be experienced as visual events within a multitextured landscape.

Phase One of the Glenstone project incorporated two important examples of modernist architecture: a private residence and a museum building (opened to the public in 2006) designed by the firm Gwathmey Siegel & Associates. Both buildings were placed at the same elevation on opposite sides of a restored pond; whereas the residence side is designed with a stacked stone wall that makes the house appear to sit slightly higher than the museum, the museum's lawn rolls gently toward the pond into a soft cluster of wetland plants.

The setting for each outdoor sculpture was specifically enhanced to facilitate installation. Richard Serra's "Contour 290" (2004) is a 15-foot-tall curving piece of weatherproof steel that extends 200 feet into a large meadow. The steel traces the contour of the land at an elevation of 290 feet, giving the piece its name. Tony Smith's painted aluminum "Smug" (1973) sits in a large, flat clearing, framed by adjacent forest. Ellsworth Kelly's matte stainless steel totem "Untitled" (2005) rises vertically at the edge of the pond, its mirrored surface reflecting dynamic changes in weather and sky. Andy Goldsworthy's stone huts—"Clay Houses (Boulder-Room-Holes)" (2007)—are made with

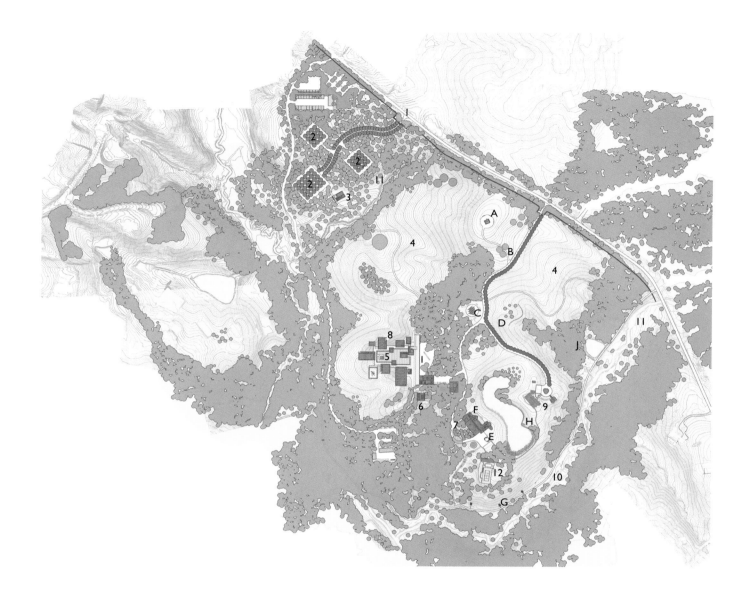

133

ART AND LANDSCAPE PLAN

A	Jeff Koons, "Split-Rocker"
B	Charles Ray, "Father Figure"
C	Tony Smith, "Smug"
D	Richard Serra, "Contour 290"
E	Richard Serra, "Sylvester"
F	Felix Gonzalez-Torres, "Untitled"
G	Andy Goldsworthy, "Clay Houses"
H	Ellsworth Kelly, "Untitled"
I	Michael Heizer, "Compression Line" (Phase II)
J	Julian Schnabel, "Untitled"

1	Entry
2	Parking Groves
3	Arrival Gallery
4	Great Meadow
5	Courtyard Water Garden
6	The Café
7	The Gallery
8	The Pavilions
9	Residence
10	Sculpture Walk and Equestrian Trail
11	Creek
12	Pool House

top left: Wooded area with Julian Schnabel sculpture group

right: Andy Goldsworthy's "Clay Houses"

bottom left: Tony Smith's "Smug"

right: Richard Serra's "Sylvester"

clay excavated nearby and nestled into the woods along the public equestrian trail at the site's lowest elevation. "Untitled" (1992) by Felix Gonzalez-Torres consists of twinned water-filled marble basins that gently touch to form a figure eight. These "pools" sit on the edge of the museum terrace and overlap the adjacent lawn to create dialogue between the built and natural environments. Finally, Jeff Koons' "Split-Rocker" (2000) is a living sculpture that embodies Glenstone's integration of the natural and man-made. Composed of thousands of individual plants growing outwards from a 40-foot structural armature, the piece sits at the site's

highest elevation point and serves as a visual touchstone for visitors below.

Each element of design and construction has emphasized a sustainable approach to achieve the highest visual impact and performance. Early on, Glenstone joined the EPA's Green Power Leadership Circle Club by purchasing renewable energy to offset electricity usage, and all general site maintenance continues to be performed using organic products. More than 1,500 new trees have been planted to develop and enhance native habitat, their success evidenced by a growing population of nesting Eastern Bluebirds. Two hundred

previously existing trees, ranging in size from 5- to 30-inch-caliper, were moved, stored, and replanted instead of replaced; and small new trees were shipped from regional nurseries to limit energy wasted in transit. The dry-stacked construction of the pond's stone wall was structured to let water percolate into the pond, thus allowing stones to shift over time without destroying the overall structure. The main lawn slopes toward the pond, facilitating the collection and storage of surface and roof run-off from all buildings to serve as irrigation water—although the surrounding woodlands and native meadows have been designed to thrive

even with no long-term irrigation. More than 17 additional acres of mown pasture and lawn have been transformed into native perennial and grass meadows, which slow run-off and require no irrigation and little general maintenance. Pervious paving has been implemented throughout the site, further enabling the water table to recharge naturally.

top left: Charles Ray's "Father Figure"

right: Ellsworth Kelly's "Untitled" at edge of pond

bottom: Jeff Koons' "Split-Rocker"

right: Felix Gonzales-Torres' "Untitled" on gallery terrace

136   REFORESTED STREAM
CORRIDOR
    TRANSPLANTED SYCAMORE –
MAIN PATH
    KNOLL

SECTION OF PAVILIONS
PHASE TWO LANDSCAPE

PHASE TWO

In 2011 Glenstone embarked upon a major expansion project, working closely with PWP to develop a site of more than 250 acres. Primary goals included selecting the location for a new museum building by architects Thomas Phifer and Partners, as well as identifying desirable adjacent properties that could productively support an expanded site plan. Together with Phifer's office and Glenstone, PWP conceived a new kind of museum landscape, one that envelops visitors from the moment they arrive, encouraging them to set aside everyday concerns and facilitating their enjoyment of art and architecture in an integrated natural environment.

Visitors will now approach Glenstone via a small county road, edged by restored woodlands, and enter the property at a clearing surrounded by a simple stacked-stone wall. The woodlands—made principally of the liriodendrons that dominate area forests—line the arrival road, leading cars to one of three parking "groves." Each parking grove is composed as a grid, planted with a different major species found in the surrounding forest: red oak, swamp white oak, and, in the main parking grove, sycamore. Seasonally the groves will be distinguished by fall color, early leaves, or peeling white bark—highlighting the complexity and dynamism of the forest as it changes throughout the year.

Visitors are invited to leave their cars and walk to the nearby Arrival Gallery, where they check in and orient themselves for their continuing visit.

From the Arrival Gallery they cross a small footbridge over a newly restored creek and emerge into a rolling meadow punctuated by specimen trees and outdoor sculpture. The new Phifer-designed building, called The Pavilions, first appears from a distance as a cluster of simple masonry forms varying in size and embedded on a landscape rise. These volumes are created to house art from Glenstone's collection and are connected below grade via a central pathway. Together The Pavilions encircle a rectangular water garden planted with water lilies, irises, and rushes. One pavilion contains only a single bench, facing outwards toward the landscape and over-looking a grove of deciduous trees atop a distant knoll. This space is devoted to quiet reflection and contemplation—offering welcome respite from "museum fatigue." Repeat visits will encourage an appreciation of Glenstone's vast demonstration of seasonal change.

Consistently prioritizing ecologically responsible practices, PWP's overall landscape design integrates walking paths, bridges, and restored woodlands with more than 6,000 trees on the expanded site and includes approximately 33 acres of existing pasture that will be developed into sustainable meadows. A collaboration with an agricultural consultant has helped integrate a natural conditioning process for existing soils during the construction process by the careful management of large grazing animals on top of stockpiled soil. Stone for landscape elements site-wide has been sourced at a nearby quarry.

top left: Entrance path to
The Pavilions

top right: View to knoll from
the gallery of The Pavilions

bottom left: Jeff Koons' "Split-
Rocker"

bottom right: Ponorama of
the Pavilions

facing page: Entry drive

*Water gardens at various
seasons of the year, from top
spring, summer, fall*

137

Newport Beach Civic Center and Park

Newport Beach, California

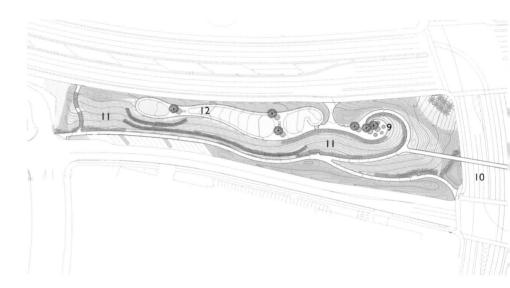

*Opening celebration on
Civic Green, 2013*

The Newport Beach Civic Center and Park is located on a 16-acre site at the center of Newport Beach. With spaces for governmental and social activities that are both functional and symbolically charged, it also lies at the very heart of the community.

At the south, the heavily visited Central Library with its new expansion and entrance by Bohlin Cywinski Jackson is located at the head of the Civic Green, which is bordered on the west side by City Hall and on the east by a two-story formal hedge masking a new parking structure. The perfect ceremonial gathering place, the Civic Green transitions—via a mixed-use plaza—to the park, which opened in 2014. It is made up of multiple meadows, habitat for native flora and fauna, meandering

trails, bridges over an existing wetland, and extensive native California-coastal planting. The water-conscious approach to planting design results in an array of native and acclimated plant communities that provide a diverse range of experiences. There are shady, sunny, wet, and dry areas, which dramatically contrast with each other and support a multitude of life forms. Bridges float over ravines. Picnic areas nestle in oaklands. At high points benches offer ocean views. Terraces for solitude hide in the desert garden.

The meandering park, in turn, transitions toward the Dog Park through what might accurately be termed a Fantasy Zone featuring a circle of white concrete rabbits with colorful eyes, perfect for children's physical and mental play.

LANDSCAPE PLAN
OF CIVIC CENTER
AND PARK

1	City Hall
2	Civic Green
3	Library
4	Garage
5	Arrival Plaza
6	Existing Wetland

7	Giant Bunny
8	Bunny Ring
9	View Terrace
10	View Bridge
11	Pine Woods
12	Dog Park
13	Meadow
14	Succulent Specimen Garden
15	Constructed Wetland

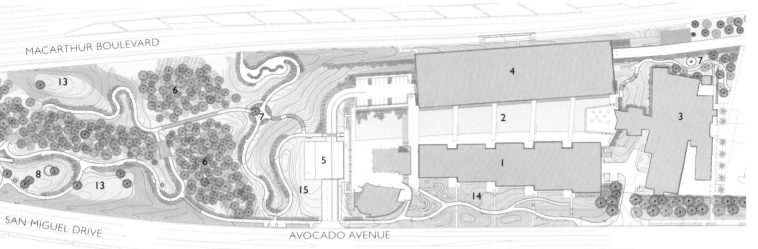
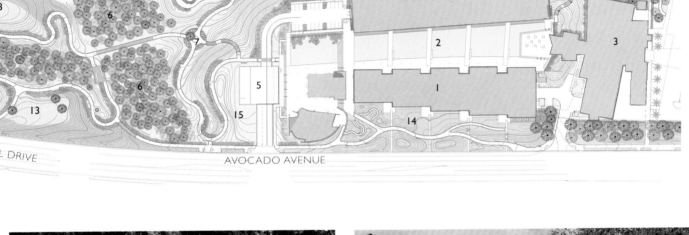

Bridge over restored wetland

Dog Park

Bunny circle

Big eight-foot bunny

145

The Dog Park fence is designed to be more than a way to keep dogs in. Rather, it is a landmark located on a hill so that people will experience it when they are simply driving by. The grove around the Dog Park is the largest mass planting of the nearly extinct Southern California native Torrey pine.

Rolling hills and the pine groves separate park activity from the adjacent boulevards. Park and Dog Park are linked by a series of meandering paths. Custom-designed furniture punctuates the park, providing refinement and coherence within a wilder setting. Transplanted palms from the previous City Hall site are an example of the conservation of resources and highlight the California horticultural heritage of the city.

The existing site required significant technical effort to realize successful horticultural conditions. Integrated design practices include on-site stormwater treatment with extensive swales and retention basins realized with planting. Throughout, the use of turf has been limited to the social heart of the project; it grows on an engineered soil that collects subdrainage water and sends it to the wetland. The nearby Fashion Island development offers an illuminating comparison. Designed in the 1960s and 1970s by SWA, it relied on manicured tropical plants and expansive lawn for visual impact. By contrast the Newport Civic Center landscape achieves its impact using form and color from native and acclimated species such as the agaves and low-water succulents on the edge planting.

Desert gardens

New York, New York

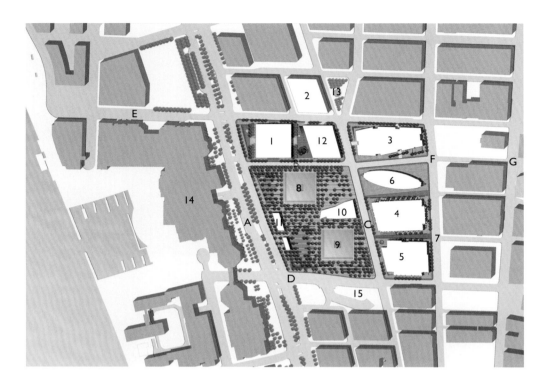

top: Ground Zero after attack, 2002

bottom: Ground Zero after cleanup, 2004

WORLD TRADE CENTER DISTRICT PLAN

1	Freedom Tower
2	Tower Seven
3	Tower Two
4	Tower Three
5	Tower Four
6	Path Station
7	Cortlandt Way
8	North Pool
9	South Pool
10	Museum Entry Pavilion
11	West Vent Structure
12	Future Performing Arts Center
13	Silverstein Park
14	World Financial Center
15	St. Nicholas Church

A	West Street
B	Fulton Street
C	Greenwich Street
D	Liberty Street
E	Vesey Street
F	Church Street
G	Broadway

The Memorial commemorates the victims of the attacks of September 11, 2001, at the World Trade Center, Shanksville, Pennsylvania, and the Pentagon, as well as the victims of the World Trade Center attack of February 26, 1993. PWP joined Michael Arad in the final stage of the 2003-2004 design competition with a mandate from the jury to humanize the scheme without diminishing the abstraction that had established it as a finalist; this humanization included making the space a park as well as a memorial, a mandate from Michael Bloomberg, New York City mayor from 2002 to 2014 and chairman of the National September 11 Memorial Foundation.

The broad scope of the trauma of the attacks required that the Memorial use a symbolic language understood by a diverse audience, a language that became an integral part of "Reflecting Absence." The two voids are placed where the destroyed towers stood. Each void is one-acre square and cut 25 feet down into the site—in a form reminiscent of Michael Heizer's "North, East, South, West" (1967/2002). Each is lined with waterfalls designed by Dan Euser and made visible at night with lighting designed by Paul Marantz of Fisher Marantz Stone.

The experience of the Memorial follows a pattern not unlike that recorded long ago by mythologist Joseph Campbell in *The Hero with a Thousand Faces* (The Bollingen Foundation, 1949).

Visitors leave the everyday life of the bustling city and enter into a mysterious zone, in this case a dense forest of 416 swamp white oak trees. Above the limbed-up trunks, a canopy of leaves provides welcome shade in the heat of summer and seasonal color in fall. In winter the sun casts shadows through a light tracery of bare branches, and in spring the trees express the renewal of nature—and life. The Memorial trees resemble an "irregular" forest, until visitors discover that in one orientation the trees align into corridors, a form recalling the arches architect Minoru Yamasaki placed at the bottom of the towers. In this way the trees express the shared patterns of nature and culture while they create a zone removed from everyday life.

left: Names of victims on low parapet beneath the plaza in original Arad scheme

top: Stone plaza in Arad's semifinalist submission

bottom: Michael Heizer's "North, East, South, West" (1967/2002), Dia Beacon, Beacon, New York

top right: Trees as a natural forest viewed from the north-south axis

bottom: Trees in colonnades viewed from the east-west axis

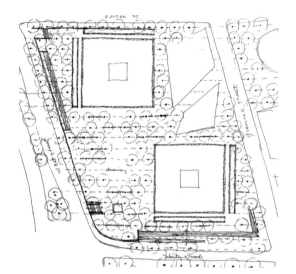

First PWP sketch of Memorial plaza/park, January 2004

LANDSCAPE PLAN OF MEMORIAL

1   North Pool
2   South Pool
3   Northeast Corner Plaza
4   The Glade
5   Survivor Tree
6   Museum Entrance/
    Pavilion
7   West Vent Structure
8   Cortlandt Street
9   Freedom Tower
10 Future Performing
    Arts Center
11 Tower Two
12 Path Station
13 Tower Three
14 Tower Four

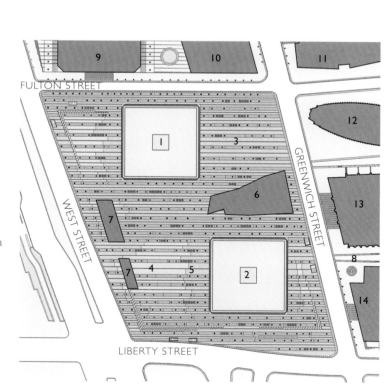

Visitors move through the forest and reexperience their grief by viewing and touching the victims' names on the bronze parapets of the voids as they listen to the thundering waterfalls. Absence—and tragedy—are rendered visible and audible, but after remembering the tragedy, visitors may take comfort from the soothing, life-affirming trees as they move back through the forest and once again join the ongoing daily life of the city. In this pattern, the overwhelming losses of September 11 are given a permanent presence in the scheme of life—an acceptance of tragedy that brings with it some degree of comfort.

In the initial design visitors descended on ramps to a space some 25 feet below the surface of the plaza to encounter the names of the victims—a profound experience but one that generated fears about security. Since any effective screening process would ruin the experience, the underground portion was eliminated and the names were moved up to the surface. In subsequent years Arad worked on the bronze panels and an ingenious system for listing the names, while PWP concentrated on the design of the plaza.

In addition to their role in creating the experience of remembering, mourning, and moving on, the trees are integral to the basic working of the design of the voids. Through their trunks the flat plane of the park is visible in its entirety. The density of the trunks extends the apparent depth and size of the plane and at the same time softens the view of the buildings beyond. Similarly, the

top: Rendering of final Memorial design proposal

bottom: 1/8-scale model to inform study of trees and flat surface of plaza

left: Open Memorial glade

right: glade on September 11th
reading of the names

150

Gothic detail of original towers

horizontal surfaces of the plaza—stone, ground cover, lawn, and steel grating— are patterned to assert and reinforce the flatness of the constructed plane, the necessary condition for experiencing the voids. In this way PWP made use of graphic techniques and technical solutions they had developed during the firm's long history of designing perceptually flat landscapes.

Within the Memorial grove, the varying distances between trees, the placement of benches, and the rhythm of ground-cover beds create spaces with distinct scale, character, and qualities of light, providing a soft green park for one of the most densely inhabited areas of Manhattan. Shaded space increases comfort for visitors and reduces heat absorption on the plaza. The transpiration of the many leaves cools the air throughout the district. A grassy clearing within the grove is designed to accommodate the annual reading of victims' names on September 11.

Working in collaboration with arborist Paul Cowie, PWP selected the swamp white oak as the tree species for the Memorial. Considered more disease-resistant than red or pin oaks, the swamp white oak provides the strength, longevity, and vaulted branch structure that lend a symbolic weight necessary for the Memorial. PWP developed a tightly controlled specification for advanced tree procurement and maintenance and selected each specimen for consistency in size and form, seeking straight-trunked oaks that would form sturdy columns. The trees were transported by Environmental Design to a temporary nursery in New Jersey where they were acclimated to the local climate for several years. At the nursery Bartlett Tree Experts pruned, irrigated, and fertilized the trees to create the uniformity in form and height necessary for a perfect canopy, a particularly difficult task given that the trees would be installed over a number of years.

Since the trees were grown in over-sized boxes at a nearby location, tree transport and installation had virtually no impact on their root system. The trees were simply craned onto a flatbed truck, driven into the city, and craned into planting pits within the plaza. In contrast to the typical ball-and-burlap tree-transplant process, which is limited to tight windows of time in spring and fall, the Memorial trees could be installed in batches through the seasons, in pace with plaza construction. Transport was conducted by Environmental Design, the off-loading and installation by Kelco Landscaping. Work was conducted in all seasons over a period of six years.

The PWP design process involves studying projects in a variety of scales and media. For the Memorial, models small and large were integral to establishing the scale, alignments, and relationships within the plaza. These models were also used to describe the project to stakeholders, political leaders, and the press. Full-scale mock-ups of each plaza component were integral to understanding details and proportions. For example, using full-scale mock-ups to study the performance of the water, Dan Euser developed a tapered, rounded weir that is water-and-energy efficient as well as highly visible and beautiful. Without Euser's comb-like weir the cost of the electricity necessary to pump the huge supply of water might well have rendered the project infeasible.

The plaza is built of relatively few elements and materials. A single pole, for instance, incorporates lighting and security. One type of granite is used for cobblestones, pavers, and benches. Planted ground cover is limited to

above: The trees throughout the seasons

Swamp white oak

Orchard

Trees boxed in New Jersey nursery

A boxed tree at the nursery

Moving a tree to New York

Planting a tree on site

Linear soil trenches and maintenance corridors

Trees placed in infrastructure

Partial completion at 2011 opening

153

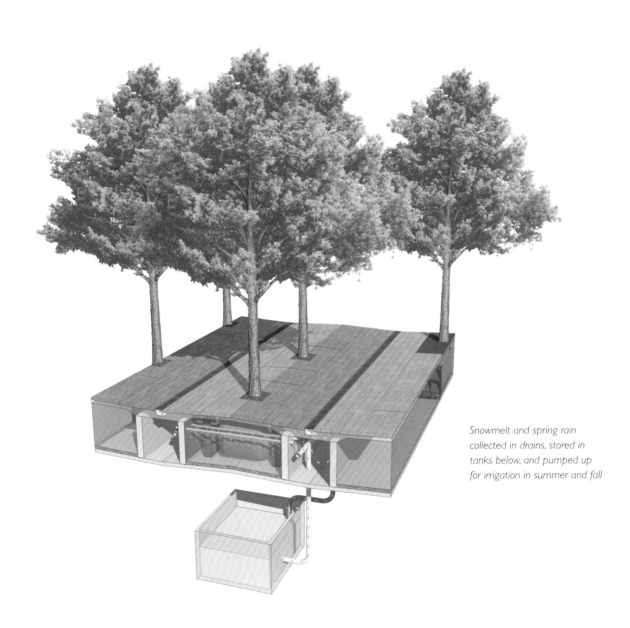

Snowmelt and spring rain
collected in drains, stored in
tanks below, and pumped up
for irrigation in summer and fall

Bench mock-ups

Full-scale paving chalked on PWP parking lot

Stainless steel drainage grill

Stone benches and paving

Stone paving set in sand

Mock-ups of lights concealing security cameras and proposed bomb-proof trash receptacles

left: *Full-scale waterfall mock-up with weir*

below: *Final waterfall weir*

evergreen English ivies and turf grass. A single tree species is repeated throughout the Memorial forest. The limited palette is critical to the notable quietness of the plaza. PWP conducted wide searches for and brought great care to the selection of each material. For example, after studying the paving pattern at full scale in chalk, PWP ultimately chose 12-inch by 60-inch pavers and 3-inch by 15-inch cobbles. The varying density of shadows in the joints between the pavers and the cobbles creates a subtle banding pattern that breaks up the vast flat plane of the Memorial into human-scaled zones. Pavers were set by hand using a sand-set paving method. Like those that make up European streets, the pavers can be lifted out and reused whenever repairs are required.

Despite its apparent simplicity, the Memorial is a massive green roof—a fully constructed integrated living system—that operates on top of multiple structures including the PATH station and tracks, the Memorial museum, a central chiller plant, parking, and additional infrastructure. One of the complications of construction was the ongoing work on projects in the five stories below the Memorial plaza as well as unfinished buildings on the periphery. Completion of some areas was delayed by almost a decade. Together with Davis Brody Bond, the associate architects for the project as well as the architects of the

museum, PWP coordinated with the Foundation and multiple agencies and governmental stakeholders to establish a consistent visitor experience.

Throughout the design and construction process, sustainability of the plaza was considered in terms of both material endurance and landscape performance. The plaza surface-and-drainage infrastructure was designed to function as a large self-sustaining cistern. Water from spring rainfall and snowmelt is channeled into large holding tanks five stories below the plaza, then filtered and stored and reused to support the Memorial forest in late summer and fall via a specialized drip-and-spray irrigation system created by Mike Astram of Northern Designs. The plaza is designed with a network of maintenance tunnels that provide access to site systems—irrigation, feeding, electrical, drainage. These tunnels will extend the life of the plaza by allowing maintenance crews to access, test, adjust, and repair both mechanical and biological systems with ease.

Substantial soil volumes—adequately irrigated, aerated, and drained—are the most critical element in the long-term success of the Memorial trees. To ensure that the oaks will grow to maturity and continue to thrive for decades an

Park at completion

First winter, 2012

above: First fall, 2011

enormous volume of soil—40,000 tons in total—lies buried in underground troughs that span the width of the plaza, soil that is bound by the maintenance tunnels and curbs at the perimeter of the project. Sod was rolled out over an engineered, compaction-resistant soil mix. PWP worked intensively with soils consultant Chuck Dixon and the testing laboratory to perfect the various blends for the lawn areas and the zones beneath the trees and within the Memorial glade.

Advanced infrastructure planning was necessary to fit together all of the buildings and streets in the district. In 2008, with towers 2, 3, and 4 in advanced stages of design—and well in advance of the establishment of the Port Authority's streets-and-sidewalks engineering team—Silverstein Properties commissioned PWP to establish a design framework for the public spaces

of the entire district. Detailed elevations set the levels of all future streets and sidewalks, building lobbies, and the Memorial. Existing and proposed underground utilities and infrastructure, such as the existing subway box, were analyzed and negotiated to create a final surface design.

Another important part of the rebuilding effort was Cortlandt Way, which is constructed with finely detailed stone pavements, stone seating walls, and retail and dining terraces to serve the needs of office workers and visitors to the Memorial. The significant grade change leading down to the Memorial was designed to amplify the view through the honey locust trees of Cortlandt Way and into the south void.

left: Day after opening day

right: The Survivor Tree

Opening day, 2011

left: Mementos

below left: Rubbings on opening day

right: Offering

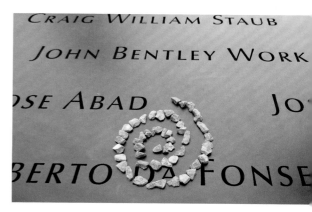

Bronze parapet with names

168

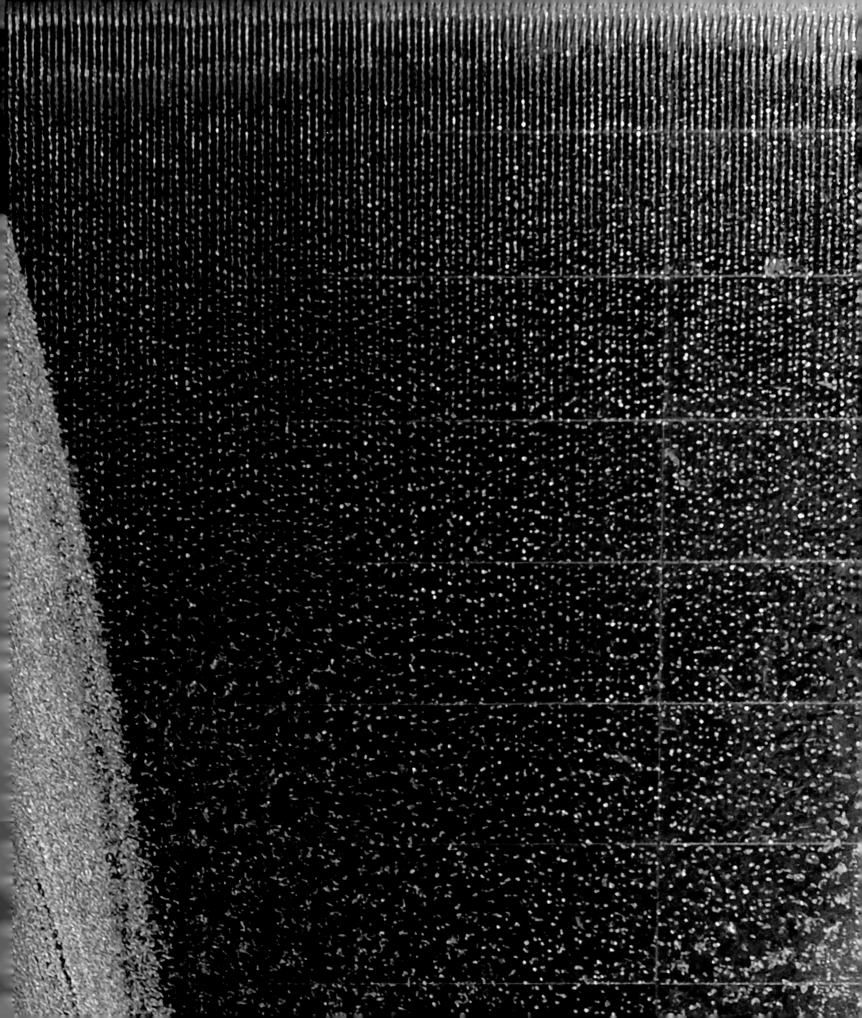

Cleveland Clinic

Cleveland, Ohio

Standing water fountain made from two acrylic walls

Over time, the campus of the Cleveland Clinic, the third largest clinic in the world and one of the top-ranking for complex heart disease, grew piecemeal, gradually encroaching upon the surrounding residential neighborhoods, where it replaced houses with surface parking lots. Cleveland has a severe climate, and pedestrian bridges connected many of the buildings so that people rarely went outdoors. A master planner had been at work prior to PWP's coming on-board in 2005, so PWP was hired under the guise of working as landscape architects within an established master plan. The planning was, however, largely based on a traffic-and-parking study that led to wider roads and a series of parking garages. The main street of town ran along the edge of the clinic with the entrance, still an automobile space, leading from the main street to the new Heart Center.

PWP proposed an alternative master plan focused on the transformation of the campus from a car-centered network to a landscape with enriched pedestrian experience. The strategy involved

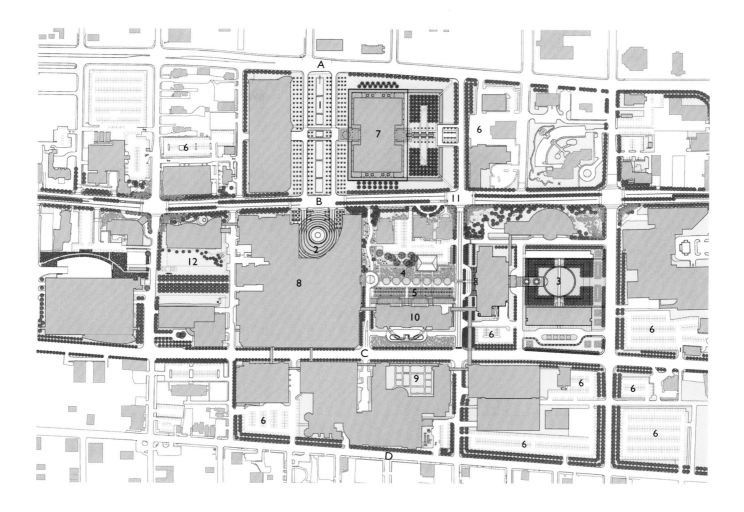

- removing public streets while maintaining necessary circulation patterns;
- creating green north-south pedestrian connections with east-west mid-block gardens;
- establishing a new arrival allée at the main entrance to the campus;
- and planting mounds to screen the existing parking lots and define the previously rough edges of campus.

The master plan also influenced the reconstruction of Euclid Avenue into a grand boulevard of trees passing through the heart of the campus. Remnant open spaces along the campus spine were aggregated to create a series of small parks for employees and patients. In 2010 Foster + Partners was hired to prepare a facilities master plan, and the landscape master plan was folded into it.

PWP's first major project consists of two main parts: an entrance allée and a large circular fountain forming a turnaround at the main entry of the Heart Center. People frequently come to the clinic in a state of anxiety so one of the highest requirements of the open space is to help create a sense of calm. In addition to patients, the clinic has some 10,000 employees, ranging from the most high-powered heart surgeons in the world to the people who take

LANDSCAPE PLAN OF CAMPUS

1 Formal Entrance Allée
2 Arrival Court with Fountain
3 Cleveland Clinic Cancer Institute
4 Crile Mall
5 Dining Grove
6 Surface Parking with Street Trees and Mounds
7 Health Education Campus
8 Heart Center
9 Lerner Courtyard
10 Hotel
11 Euclid Mall
12 West Mall

A Chester Avenue
B Euclid Avenue
C Carnegie Avenue
D Cedar Street

Grid of stones in the reflecting pools

Allée of columnar tulip poplars

care of the buildings. In the president's view, all of them should have a positive identification with the campus. Just as studies have shown that recuperation happens more quickly in landscaped surroundings, a green campus can also have a calming effect on people working for long hours under great tension. In outdoor spaces patients and employees alike can sit by themselves and read a book or sit in groups and talk or have lunch—all important releases from the intensity of medical life.

THE ALLÉE

A new symbol of the clinic, the two-block-long Allée is designed to convert a previously uneventful automobile trip past a drugstore and a 1970s strip-mall parking lot into a visually interesting experience. The Allée's width allows for a simple set of water features and a grove of trees that can be enjoyed as people move to and from the Heart Center.

The grove, composed of 298 columnar tulip trees (*Liriodendron tulipifera* 'Arnold'), frames a series of six pools through which water slowly moves, reflecting the sky. Within the pools sits a grid of 300 Wisconsin granite boulders. The trees and boulders act as strong sculptural elements that provide human scale while drawing attention to seasonal change in the largest green space on the campus.

THE HEART CENTER
ARRIVAL PLAZA

The entry is a wide, circular arrival and drop-off space, scaled to accommodate three to four lanes of traffic. Its atmosphere could conceivably be perceived as upsetting, given the scale of the place and the cacophony of arrival and departure activity. To provide a sense of calm PWP relied on a geometrically grounded centerpiece, a lighted pool—80 feet in diameter—made of two clear acrylic

circular cylinders set on a disc of broken granite, within rings of black brick pavers and gray granite cobbles. The acrylic walls of the fountain are invisible and rounded on top so that they produce a slow, elegant movement of the water, which seems to stand unsupported in the air. The water changes color and mood depending on the angles of sun and wind and the reflections of the buildings. At night the lighted pool welcomes visitors.

Samsung Seocho

Seoul, Korea

Bamboo planting

*Model of central
access road*

In 2004 Samsung commissioned PWP to design a new downtown headquarters in the center of Seoul, Korea. The design of the complex encompassed two primary goals: achieving a successful pedestrian and vehicular circulation network through the site and creating three distinctive places for the daily use of Samsung employees, their visitors, and people in the adjacent neighborhoods. The three areas are the Community Plaza, a gathering place for small groups or large events; the Corporate Park, a human-scale green garden composed of natural materials that contrast with its hard-edged urban surroundings; and the Samsung Plaza at Tower C, a large private roof garden with rusticated stonewalls to retain soil for elevated planting. At the center of the roof garden a water garden filled with a variety of water lilies, grasses, and carefully placed natural specimen boulders was designed to freeze in the winter when the plants are dormant, thereby greatly reducing energy and maintenance costs.

The client wanted a plaza with trees, pavement, benches, fountains—everything that would produce a unique place within the city.

What was particularly challenging was that construction was already more than half complete. The architect, KPF (Kohn Pederson Fox), with whom PWP has worked many times, had completed three office towers and an underground parking garage that covered the entire site, allowing only a narrow strip of planting soil along the main street. Nevertheless, using a series of raised planters, wood benches with lights, metal vine structures, varied pavements, fountains, and custom light fixtures, PWP produced a memorable series of squares, entry plazas, casual lounging terraces, and executive roof gardens. To cope with the high density of users and visitors, this urban landscape is built with fine materials that are especially durable, requiring virtually no repair.

top: Pool and planted cage walls

bottom: Fountains at the subway entry

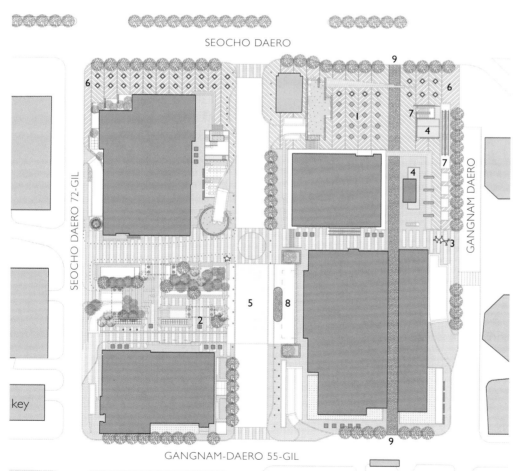

SEOCHO DAERO

SEOCHO DAERO 72-GIL

GANGNAM DAERO

GANGNAM-DAERO 55-GIL

key

STREET-LEVEL PLAN OF CENTER

1   Community Plaza
2   Corporate Park
3   Sculpture
4   Water Element
5   Samsung Plaza
6   Public Promenade
7   Subway Entrance
8   Arrival Court
9   Pedestrian Way

Wooden raised planter garden

Stair to Community Plaza

Cage "trees" planted from within

*Stone cobbled entry plaza
with metal cage "trees"*

Nasher Sculpture Center

Dallas, Texas

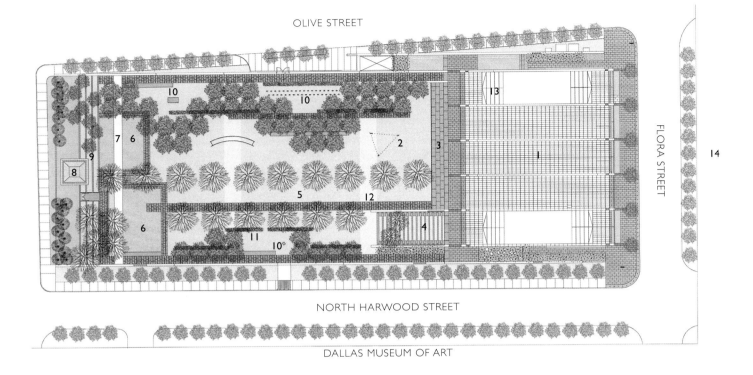

OLIVE STREET

NORTH HARWOOD STREET

DALLAS MUSEUM OF ART

FLORA STREET

188

14

GARDEN PLAN

1 Museum
2 Great Lawn
3 Porch and Stairs
4 Amphitheater
5 Live-oak Allée
6 Pool
7 Boardwalk
8 Turrell Room
9 Stepped Garden
10 Cedar-elm Rooms
11 Hedges
12 Stone Walk
13 Café
14 Asian Museum

The Nasher Sculpture Center, a gift to the citizens of Dallas from the Nasher family, features an impressive collection of modern sculpture for both indoor and outdoor viewing. Raymond Nasher built up the collection with his wife, Patsy R. Nasher, and continued collecting after her death in 1988. From 1999 to 2004 PWP created an outdoor gallery that is home to several permanent pieces and features 20 to 30 others in changing exhibits.

The garden design extends Renzo Piano's building, a parallel series of "archaeological" walls that allow views from Flora Street (the main street of the Arts District) through the delicately glazed building and out to the garden. Display spaces are created by live-oak allées, cedar-elm bosques, rows of holly hedges, and a series of stone plinths that serve as seating and pedestals for sculpture. The plinths also hold flexible systems of lighting, sound, and irrigation. As a counterpoint to the linear display space, the cedar elms create more intimate outdoor rooms for sculpture of different scales.

Fountains and pools at the side and end of the garden attract the eye and mask adjacent automobile noise. At the side of the building fine sparkling jets originating in the garden wall rain into a 70-foot-long pool planted with water

lilies. At the foot of the garden, two pools with lines of white-water jets and a linear planting of rushes draw visitors through the garden. A sculpture room by James Turrell is embedded in an eight-foot-high mound behind the pool area. It is planted with a loose grove of pine that forms a backdrop for a drift of flowering crape myrtle. Groves of bamboo and rows of magnolias frame the sides of the building.

Creating a sculpture garden with both permanent and changing exhibits comes with some challenges, specifically the need to use mechanical equipment to move large, heavy pieces and site them within the garden. This requirement necessitated the invention of a special soil system that supports weight, drains perfectly without catch basins, and encourages the growth of a resilient turf grass as well as the many specimen trees. Pavement was made of flame-finish dark Verde Fontaine granite with green highlights that echo the deep green of the garden. Although beautiful, it was kept to a minimum, allowing easy access through the full extent of the garden and thus encouraging use of the lawns for viewing the artwork and for large openings and special functions.

A few of the more than 200 civic events that take place each year

*Spaces for sculpture formed
by clipped holly hedges*

Cedar-elm bosques

*facing page: A quiet pool
at the foot of the garden*

Colorado Esplanade

Santa Monica, California

PLAN OF ESPLANADE AND EXPO LINE STATION

1   Downtown Light-Rail Station
2   Crosswalk Plaza
3   Promenade Paving
4   Gateway Triangle
5   To Santa Monica Civic Center
6   To Downtown Santa Monica
7   To Santa Monica Pier

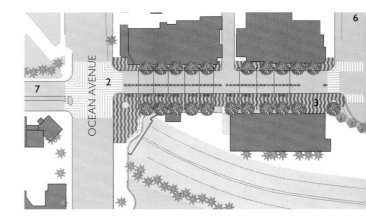

The Colorado Esplanade was conceived by the City of Santa Monica as a vital urban-design element that conveys the spirit of the city. A three-block-long linear plaza along Colorado Boulevard between the new light-rail station on Fourth Street and the historic Santa Monica Pier, the project (which began for PWP in 2011) is not only intended to deliver pedestrians coming from the light-rail to the coast, but also to connect downtown Santa Monica in the north with Santa Monica's Civic Center district in the south, across the freeway. Thus, the Colorado Esplanade will be a multimodal thoroughfare that connects thousands of people to all corners of Santa Monica every day.

Initially these aspirational goals seemed impossible to achieve because the space available for the project was little more than a sidewalk streetscape. PWP, in collaboration with a team of professionals, City staff, and the people of Santa Monica, was able to find surprising efficiencies that allow for a design communicating the identity of Santa Monica and offering a multimodal route for travelers of all kinds.

Early in the analysis and planning phases of the project PWP asked if it was possible to turn the stretch of Colorado Boulevard into a one-way street, posing the question to Fehr and Peers, the traffic consultants for the project, who had a long history of studying traffic issues in Santa Monica. Together, the team hypothesized that turning Colorado to a one-way street running west for the length of the Esplanade would allow one existing lane of vehicular paving to be transformed into pedestrian and cycling zones. Removing a lane of vehicular traffic was a radical notion because Santa Monica (and the greater Los Angeles area) has perennial traffic problems. There seemed to be little chance of gaining traction. Fehr and Peers,

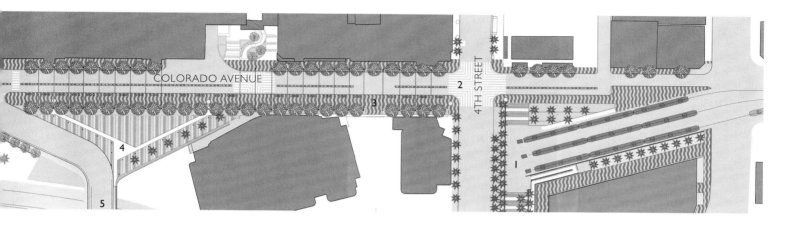

COLORADO AVENUE

4TH STREET

2

3

4

1

5

Esplanade at night and during the day

Cross-over plazas at major intersections

Esplanade looking toward the historic Santa Monica Pier sign

Festival paving in front of retail

Sidewalk passage glowing in the evening hours

however, reviewed the scheme and ran traffic models of the entire downtown area with the changed street. Surprisingly to many, it was determined that changing the boulevard to a one-way street for cars actually alleviated some of the existing traffic issues within downtown Santa Monica. With this finding, PWP went through a series of public meetings and sessions with Santa Monica's City Council that ultimately resulted in the basis of the final scheme. PWP developed the final design through an extensive community engagement process with the stakeholders associated with the Esplanade, including the City Planning Department of Santa Monica as well as other City agencies and staff, Downtown Santa Monica Incorporated, adjacent property owners, and Santa Monica residents who engaged in public workshops and meetings.

Using only basic materials, the design for the Colorado Esplanade creates a shared public-space for pedestrians, cyclists, drivers, and buses. All users of the Esplanade are contained between two rows of trees that are planted at the outer edges of the space, a planted allée that focuses the view on the historic Santa Monica Pier sign (the symbolic end of Route 66). The trees—as well as string lights and their support poles—frame the entire zone and connect the north and south sides of the street.

Custom rippled-concrete unit pavers elevate the pedestrian zone and create an identity to the walk that is recognizable the moment visitors step onto it. The Esplanade is also home to Santa Monica's first bicycle track that allows cyclists to travel in both directions. The bicycle track is separated from the vehicular lanes by a three-foot-wide and six-inch-high curb; the pedestrian walkway is separated from the bicycle track by a sidewalk curb with small seating elements.

The new Gateway Triangle creates a framed entry plaza for parks at the City Hall and the Civic Auditorium. The plant palette throughout the project is strong and simple with bold street trees as well as mass plantings that offer color and fragrance.

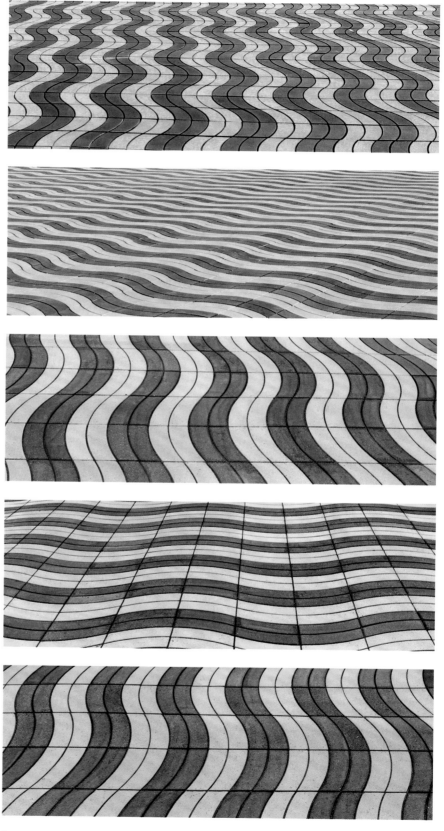

Festival paving

Marina Bay Sands
Integrated Resort

Singapore

top left: Sunset from the infinity pool

top right: Pool view toward downtown

PWP worked with Safdie Architects, the Singapore government, and a team of local landscape architects and horticulturalists, engineering and architectural consultants, and business professionals to create the landscape for Marina Bay Sands Integrated Resort. The complex of buildings and open spaces on a 40-acre site is the keystone project for the Marina Bay Peninsula, the landfill expansion to the island of Singapore that creates Singapore Bay. The overall project includes a casino, two theaters, an art and science museum, a convention center, one million square feet of retail space, and three hotel towers. Beginning in 2005, PWP was responsible for the planning and design of the outdoor public spaces that occur at all elevations in the multi-story development,

including landscape spaces around, on top of, and within the architectural structure.

Public landscapes include the 1.5-kilometer-long Waterfront Promenade; the Landscape Bridge, which crosses over two major city streets from the main building to the hotel lobby and lands in the public botanical garden; the Sky Promenade and Rooftop Piazza on top of the podium of the casino and convention-center building; the Hotel Garden, which surrounds the three hotel towers; the planted façade of the hotel towers; and the highly-vegetated streetscapes that provide pedestrian connections within the neighborhood. Of the private landscape spaces for hotel guests the most remarkable is

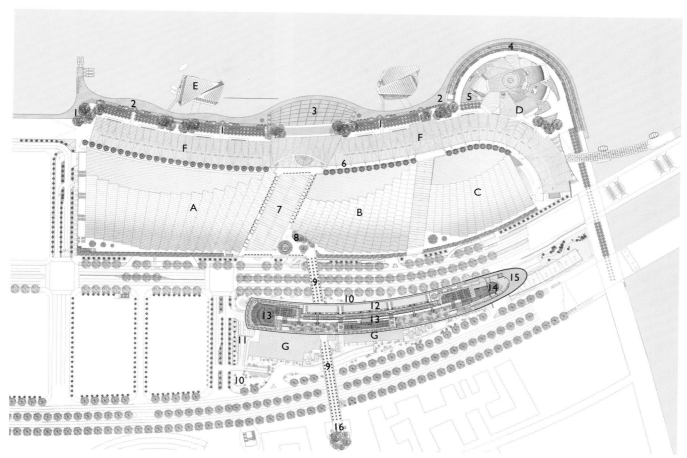

the three-acre Sky Park, which spans the 57-story hotel towers, offers 360-degree views of the sea and city, and includes a public viewing deck that is popular with tourists. The Sky Park's amenities include an infinity-edge swimming pool that is longer than three Olympic pools and a series of flagstone-paved garden rooms containing mature trees and soaking tubs. Seventy-five percent of the 30 acres of landscape in the project is public space, and virtually all is built on structure.

Given the tropical climate of Singapore—rain and heat every day—and the consequent concerns for pedestrian comfort and a range of water issues, the horticultural and ecological designs were critical to the project.

At the Waterfront Promenade, triple allées of Roystonia palms interrupted with informal groupings of large canopy trees—*Khaya senegalensis, Peltophorum, pterocarpum,* and *Alstonia scholaris*—provide a shaded walk along the water. The promenade runs parallel to the transparent façade and air-conditioned linear retail atrium, thus allowing maximum connection along with relief from the hot climate and promoting maximum waterfront use. All stormwater run-off from the promenade is collected and used to irrigate the landscape. Similarly, all streetscape planting focuses on maximizing comfort, minimizing water requirements, and reusing stormwater run-off. These water practices are in keeping with those of the City, which created the peninsula from landfill to

PLAN OF RESORT

A   Convention Center
B   Casino
C   Theaters
D   ArtScience Museum
E   Crystal Pavilions
F   Retail Mall
G   Hotel

PUBLIC LANDSCAPE

1   Waterfront Promenade
2   Boardwalk
3   Event Plaza
4   Museum Trellis
5   Lily Pond
6   Sky Promenade (Level 4)
7   Hoop Arbors (Level 4)
8   Rooftop Piazza (Level 4)
9   Sky Bridge (Level 4)
10 Hotel Garden
11 Hotel Drop Off
12 Pool Deck (Level 57)
13 Restaurants (Level 57)
14 Nightclub (Level 57)
15 Public Viewing Deck
16 Botanical Garden Overlook

Restaurant and café activity at pool

turn the salt-water bay into a reservoir that will ultimately become a freshwater catchment area. The entire project is within the Singapore Garden City Framework and the Singapore Green Plan. The design maximizes water conservation with careful selection of plant materials, strategic soil preparation, and permeable paving.

Since tree nurseries are few and carry minimal stock in this small island nation, PWP initiated a tree-procurement strategy that included the creation of a temporary nursery to enable the advance purchase and acclimatization of high-quality trees close to the site. Very large specimen trees and large quantities of trees in matched sizes were required to provide character and identity as well as pedestrian comfort. PWP tagged each tree on the basis of specific goals. More than 200 Roystonia palms for the Promenade were chosen for health and uniformity because they were intended to create a planted extension to the architecture of the Grand Arcade of the retail mall. Each was measured and assessed for similarity of form. Later, at the pregrow nursery, each palm was reassessed and ordered according

to form and height for phased installation. To contrast with the uniformity of the palm allée the large wide-crowned shade trees placed at the nodes along the Promenade had forms that were targeted to be irregular and different from, although complementary to, one another.

One argument for establishing the pregrow nursery was the effect that transportation would have on the shapes of these Promenade shade trees. Since they all came from Malaysia, they had to cross the Singapore border on tractor trailers through a gantry crossing. Thus, the trees could be no more than 15 meters long, including their root balls, and only four or five meters wide. Most would have to be severely pruned in width. A common practice in the industry in Asia, it leads to trees that are unsightly at installation. A pregrow nursery would serve as a place where the truncated trees could grow new limbs and achieve renewed health and beauty before they were delivered to the site. The argument was convincing, and, as it turned out, the phenomenal growing conditions in Singapore quickly produced mature and vibrant trees after only 18 months in the pregrow nursery.

top: Waterside boardwalk and dock

bottom: Flowering arcade

top left: Tree-lined bridge to garden by the sea

top right: Pedestrian garden

facing page: Palm-lined promenade

bottom left: Quiet terrace with ocean view

bottom right: A walk through colorful tropical plants

IN PROGRESS

Slated for completion in 2017, the Transbay Transit Center, a mul- timodal transit station that includes bus and high-speed rail, is capped at the roof with a 5.4-acre park. It has been designed as both a destination and community park within an area of downtown San Francisco undergoing tremendous growth but with little unoccupied land. Conceived of as a multifunctional space providing respite, activity, and education, the park is integrally designed with the building in order to achieve expansive areas of soil to support large, healthy trees and shrubs.

Since the park is one block wide and nearly a quarter of a mile long, its features will be experienced episodically. The design is composed of curving paths through different settings, both contemplative and social. Visitors can enter at many locations from the street level below and on bridges from buildings above, and as they move along they will come to a variety of activity areas that include a central plaza and café, a children's play area,

Transbay Transit Center and Mission Square

San Francisco, California

lookout belvederes, and—at the western end—an amphitheater and restaurant. In order to create a topography that blurs the distinction between roof and ground, the design plays mounded vegetated hills against the domed architectural skylights that channel daylight into the terminal below. PWP worked closely with environmental artist Ned Kahn on the 1,200-foot-long "Bus Jet Fountain"—a feature in which buses moving through the terminal on the fourth floor trigger jets of water in the roof park above.

The park will actively improve the environment by absorbing carbon dioxide from bus exhaust, treating and recycling water, and creating a locus in downtown San Francisco for birds, butterflies, and bees as well as people. Stormwater runoff from the park, as well as gray water from the sinks in the terminal building, will be collected and polished in a subsurface constructed wetland garden at the east end of the park. The reclaimed water will then be used in the restrooms throughout the terminal. At the ground level, PWP worked with multiple agencies to develop a streetscape and urban design for the four-block-long core of the Transbay District, including Mission Square, a new civic plaza for San Francisco. A monumental sculpture by Tim Hawkinson anchors the corner of Mission Square, and a kinetic gondola transports people from the redwood grove in the plaza up into the redwood forest in the Rooftop Park.

facing page: Aerial view

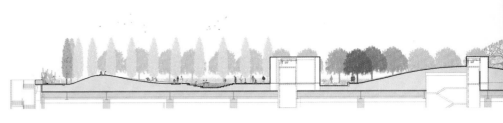

SECTION OF ROOF PARK

AMPHITHEATER RESTAURANT STAIR IN GROUND-
COVER MOUND

PLAN OF ROOF PARK

1   Main Plaza and Café
2   Arrival Grove
3   Light Column
    (Grand Hall Below)
4   Skylight
5   Picnic Meadow
6   Gondola to Mission Square
7   Mission Square
8   Bridge to Tower
9   "Bus Jet Fountain"
10 Amphitheater
11 Restaurant
12 Children's Play Area
13 Wetland Garden and Gray
    Water Treatment
14 Botanical Display Gardens
15 California Garden

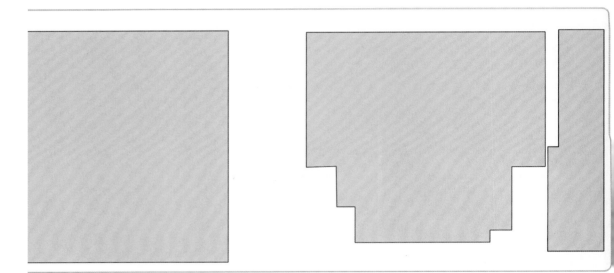

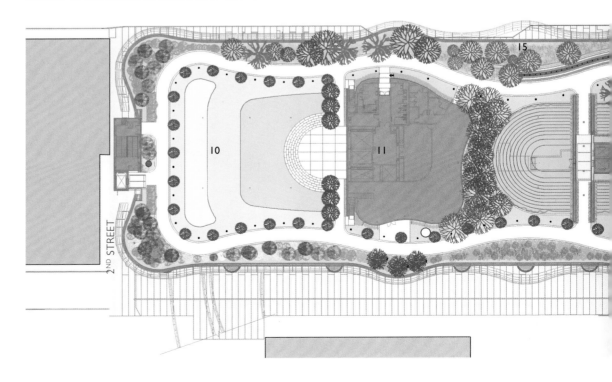

top: Ned Kahn's "Bus Jet Fountain"
on northwestern edge of park

bottom: View of park from
street level

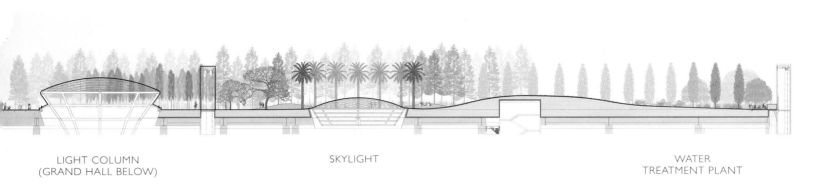

LIGHT COLUMN
(GRAND HALL BELOW)

SKYLIGHT

WATER
TREATMENT PLANT

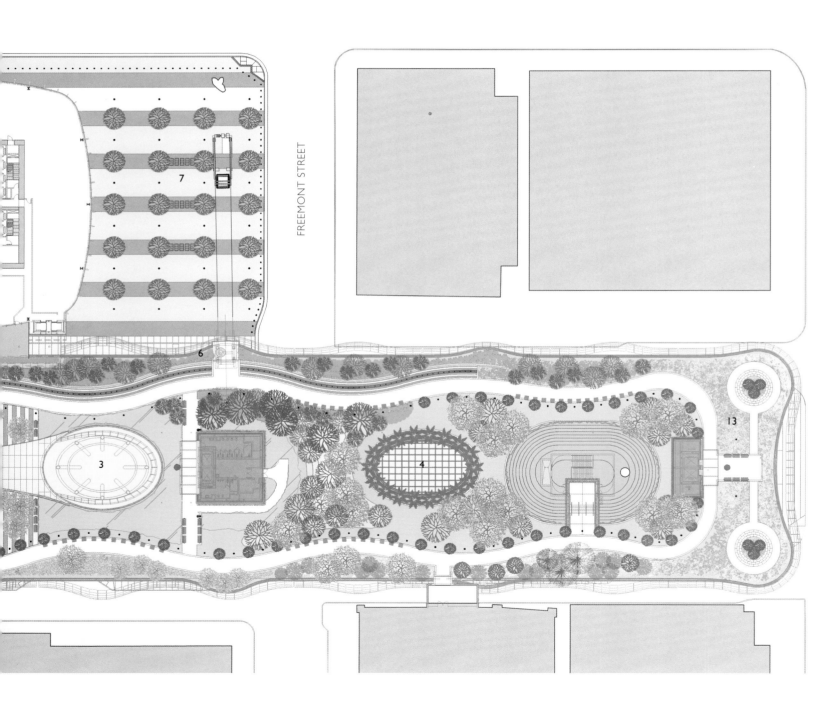

FREEMONT STREET

7

6

3

4

13

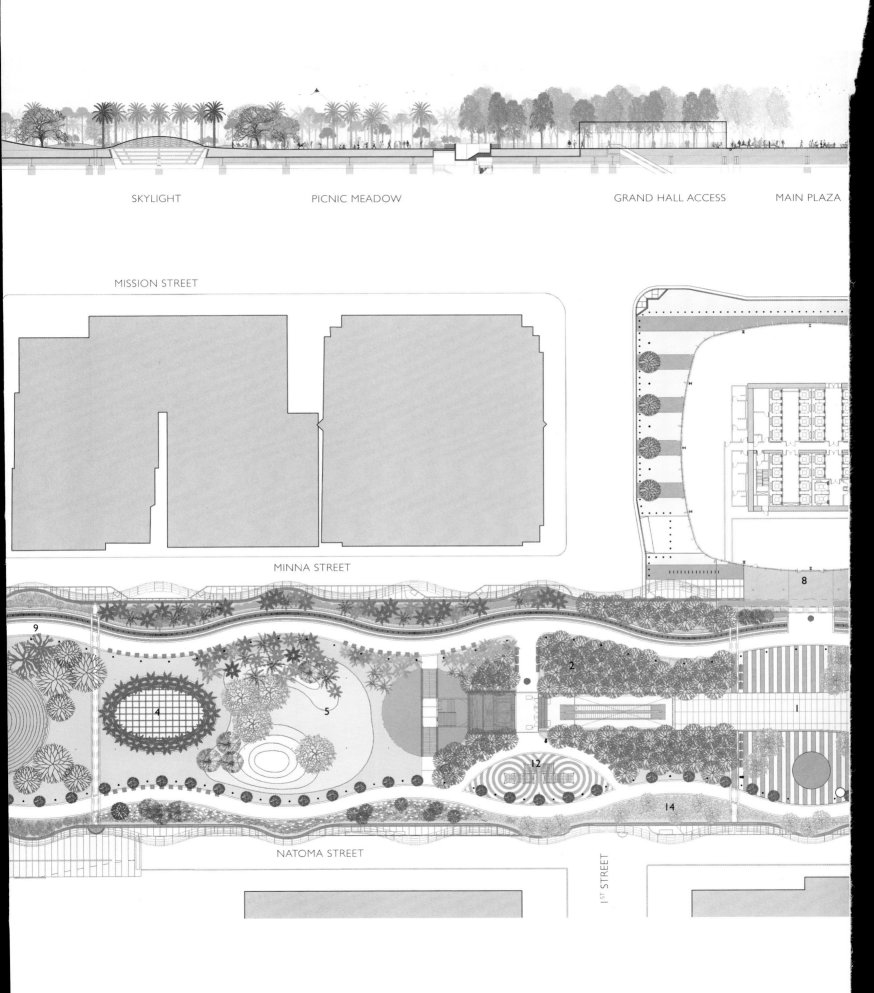

SKYLIGHT   PICNIC MEADOW   GRAND HALL ACCESS   MAIN PLAZA

MISSION STREET

MINNA STREET

NATOMA STREET

1ST STREET

9

2

4

5

1

12

8

14

BUS DECK WITH   REDWOOD   FUNICULAR   MISSION STREET
PARK ABOVE   GROVE   TO PARK

SECTION OF MISSION SQUARE

top: Escalator entrance pavilion

bottom: Woods at park level

Khiran Pearl City Marina

Khiran, Kuwait

above: Aerial view of arrival garden and parking

Located south of Kuwait City on the Persian Gulf, the new resort community of Sabah Al Ahmed Sea City is projected to have a population of up to 200,000 people living along 70 kilometers of inland waterways. Tamdeen Group is developing the commercial center of the new community, which includes a 75,000-square-meter retail mall, three high-rise residential towers, a major park, and a five-star hotel placed around a 900-slip marina, the country's largest.

A 1.6-kilometer promenade, defined by four rows of palms, illuminated custom seating, and lighted runnels, links the entire development around the marina and features restaurant terraces,

fountains, event spaces, and gardens as well as walking and seating areas. Fabric sails among the palm trees provide additional shade for the dining terraces and walking paths. The promenade is defined by a foreshore walk lined with six-meter-tall perforated steel lighting columns filled with glass rock that casts an aqua glow around the marina.

The central feature of the development is the Pearl, a 2.7-hectare public destination park extending into the middle of the marina. A monumental ten-meter-high viewing mound is surrounded by gardens, custom-designed play areas, public art, an outdoor performance and multimedia stage, amphitheater

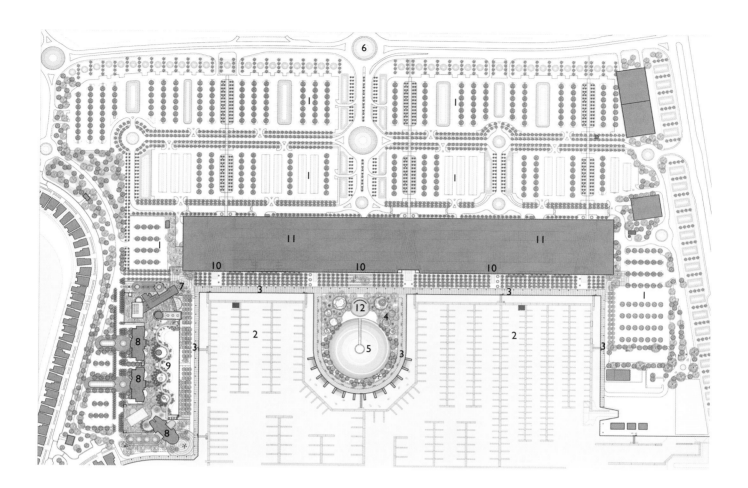

Street-side view with deciduous grass mounds and rows of palms

PLAN OF RETAIL COMPLEX

1   Parking
2   Marina
3   Marina Promenade
4   Playground
5   Lookout Green
6   Grand Arrival
7   Hotel
8   Residences
9   Beach Garden
10 Restaurants
11 Shopping Mall
12 Stage

top: Translucent shade structures within palm allées

bottom: Hotel entrance

seating, and jogging and walking paths. A 400-meter-long covered trellis along the foreshore walk provides protective cover for seating with views into the park and out to the marina. At night the trellis casts a white glow around the Pearl.

A three-story garden podium links the three residential towers and the hotel. The major feature of the residential and hotel gardens is a 151-meter-long infinity pool and sand beach with

dramatic views into the marina and inland waterways. Cafes, dining terraces, play areas, garden paths, and tennis courts fill the garden landscape.

The parking areas have been designed into a series of arrival gardens using extensive low-water-use plantings. Covered walkways and a variety of palms and canopy trees serve as wayfinding to the entrances of the retail mall.

above: Marina-side palm promenade

University of Texas at Austin

Austin, Texas

AERIAL VIEW OF CAMPUS

 Original Forty Acres

 Speedway corridor and
East Mall

Many of America's great universities were conceived as idealized cities, the most memorable possessing a spatial harmony that symbolically expresses the process of rational thought and invites contemplation—for example, the academic cores of such campuses as the University of Virginia, Stanford, and Harvard. Among these great spaces is the academic core of the University of Texas at Austin, called the Original Forty Acres. Designed by Paul Cret at the turn of the last century, this highly integrated, well-defined landscape is composed of courtyards and buildings arrayed in careful harmony reminiscent of the Spanish Renaissance.

In the last half of the twentieth century the integrity of many great American campuses began to erode. The Cret landscape proved no exception. As the car became a necessary part of the operation of the campus, roads, driveways, and loading docks gained visual prominence over such pedestrian spaces as allées, lawns, and terraces. Yet the center of the campus still offers glimpses of the original order and harmony. Huge trees grace hedge-lined greens; seat walls surround lushly planted beds; students sit on low walls and steps along well-scaled paths, free of cars. The purpose of the remodeling of the Speedway corridor and the East Mall is to extend the order of the Original Forty Acres to the structural framework of the modern campus.

215

top: Nancy Rubins' "Monochrome for Austin" at the Norman Hackerman Building

middle: Commission of 125 Plaza with dining terrace beyond

bottom: Festival activity at the Gregory Gymnasium Plaza

**SITE PLAN OF SPEEDWAY
AND EAST MALL**

1   Pedestrian Promenade
2   Fountain (Future)
3   Arrival Plaza
4   Austin Green
5   East Mall
6   Ellsworth Kelly, "Austin"
7   Blanton Museum Court
8   Gregory Gymnasium Plaza
9   Commission of 125 Plaza
10   Outdoor Café
11   Engineering Allée
12   To Main Building
13   Waller Creek
14   Gregory Gym
15   Welch Hall
16   Blanton Museum of Art

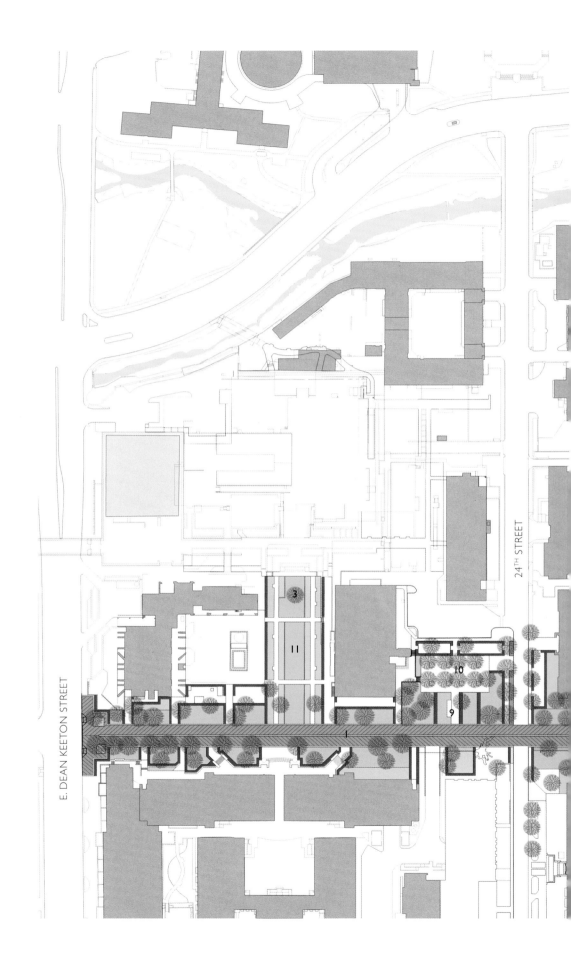

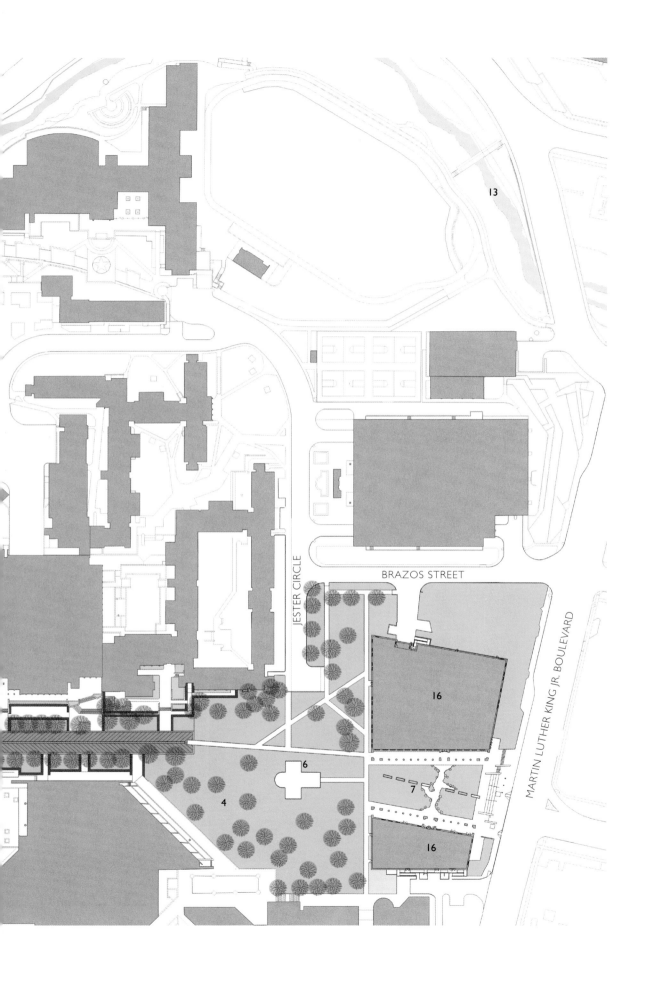

JESTER CIRCLE

BRAZOS STREET

MARTIN LUTHER KING JR. BOULEVARD

13

16

16

6

4

7

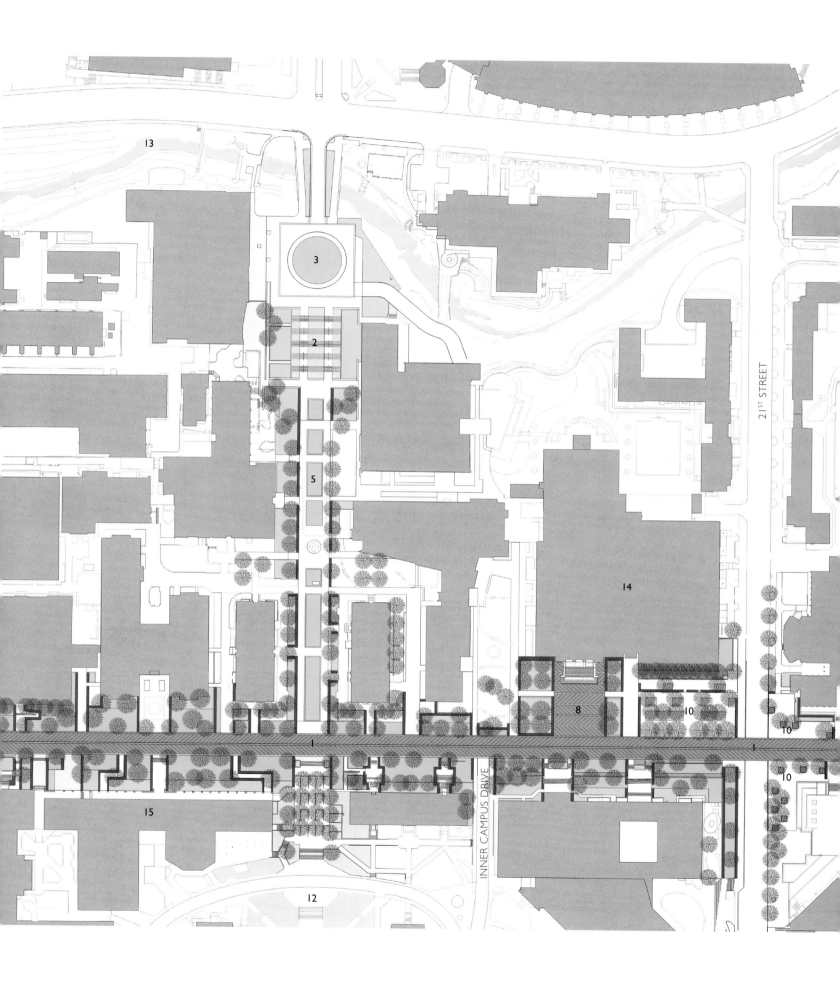

13

3

2

5

14

8

10

10

1   1

10

15

INNER CAMPUS DRIVE

21ST STREET

12

Food truck café at corner of Speedway and 21st Street

217

left: Looking down Speedway on a busy afternoon

At its southern precinct, framed by the two buildings of the Blanton Museum, Speedway gives a view of the State Capitol to the south, a reference to the status of the university. Just to the north of the Blanton, sitting within a green meadow, is "Austin" by Ellsworth Kelly. PWP collaborated with the Kelly team on the integration of the piece within Speedway. The corridor itself will be narrowed to a pedestrian-friendly 30 feet wide. It will be paved in a mellow golden sand-molded brick referencing the warm golden brick that characterizes the traditional campus architecture. On each side, the space gained by narrowing the corridor will be lined with green lawns and shady trees. Rows of hedges reminiscent of the original historic quad will run perpendicular to Speedway and divide these dappled lawns into intimate spaces for conversation and study while providing settings for permanent artwork or

temporary student sculpture exhibitions. Set back from the walk, broad beds of ground cover will soften the edges of the large academic buildings. Gaps in the current tree cover will be planted to increase shade, largely with live oaks.

At Speedway's major intersections with 21st and 24th streets, new outdoor plazas will provide gathering places with food trucks and tables and chairs of a character to encourage social interaction. All will be shaded with umbrellas or orchard-like trees with the upper canopies gradually filling in to protect against the Texas sun. The large entry plazas at Perry Castaneda Library and Gregory Gymnasium will be replanted and configured more closely to the new human scale of Speedway.

above: Model of proposed
stepped fountain at East Mall

In a proposed scheme for the center of the East Mall, which stretches east from the Original Forty Acres toward the Lyndon Baines Johnson Library, wide seat-height beds of simple lawn would rise between the rows of existing oaks, providing places for informal repose, without inviting the spontaneous passages that cut unsightly desire lines across the existing grass. The dense canopies of the East Mall oaks would be trimmed to allow more sun on the green surfaces below.

Where East Mall tips toward Waller Creek, Paul Cret initially envisioned an amphitheater settled into the natural topography, within earshot of running water, and shaded by riparian vegetation. Today, this spot has become the largest single entry point to the campus, the primary student-commuter-bus drop-off just across Waller Creek at the football stadium. An overly monumental baroque fountain with walls stained by age currently blocks the western movement, its stairs running counter to the natural flow of foot traffic toward the central campus. The proposed East Mall Entry would replace this fountain with a wide cascade of running water interspersed by two broad bands of stone steps. The cascade steps would glow at night, leading the eye to the tower at the top of the hill beyond.

right: Model of proposed automobile arrival plaza at East Mall

219

Proposed East Mall and
stepped fountain at night

China Resources

Shenzhen Bay, China

*above: Private educational terrace
and residential garden on roof of
the shopping mall*

China Resources at Shenzhen Bay
is a composite development for the
headquarters of China Resources
Company Limited. Located in a des-
ignated new central business district
of Shenzhen, the project comprises
a 400-meter-high China Resources
headquarters tower and museum by
KPF; a 180-meter-high China Resources
Vanguard headquarters building and
luxury hotel by Goettsch Partners;
and more than 100,000 square meters
of residential and high-end shopping
mall by RTKL. The landscape master
plan helped tie the different parcels of

the development into a comprehen-
sive precinct with an emphasis on the
pedestrian zone and outdoor amenities
and activities.

PWP worked closely with KPF on the
site plan for the headquarters tower
and museum. The landscape knits the
tower landscape to the larger precinct
through common materials such as
stone paving, custom light fixtures,
and street-tree planting. A grid of
Delonix regia (flame tree) and custom
benches set within a large lawn in the
central park spill out to the pavilion
and headquarters tower.

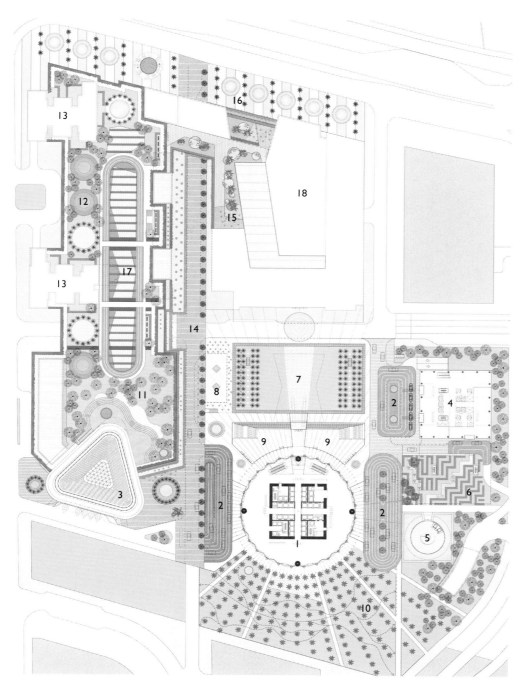

*top: Rooftop swim club
at residential towers*

*bottom: Running track at
residential roof garden*

The Vanguard Tower rooftop and hotel were designed in collaboration with Goettsch Partners. The rooftop landscape provides areas for small outdoor classes or informal gatherings with amphitheater seating and small stages surrounded by lush gardens.

The streetscapes and pedestrian plazas surrounding RTKL's shopping mall are integrated into the precinct with the use of common materials, lighting, and planting. Close coordination was required to incorporate the large skylights in the shopping mall into the rooftop landscape and to screen the unsightly mechanical systems. The rooftop provides gardens, intimate spaces, and a running track for residents of the high-end residential towers.

*top: Sunken amphitheater
with lower entry to headquarters,
museum, and mall*

*middle: Museum entry garden
at headquarters arrival plaza*

*bottom: Dining pavilion at
central park*

Kuwait International Tennis Complex

Kuwait City, Kuwait

The Kuwait International Tennis Complex is a mixed-use destination development that includes retail, a Grand Hyatt Hotel, a health club, and an arena as well as a tennis complex and the headquarters of the Kuwait Tennis Federation. Located on the Sixth Ring Road of Kuwait City, the development is an extension of the successful 360 Mall, a huge high-end retail and entertainment complex.

Occupying the eastern approach to the development is the Foreground Park, a landscape consisting of mounded roadway islands overlaid with a radial pattern of grass and stone bands emanating outward from the tennis complex drop-off. The tennis complex is designed to host professional tournaments with eight outdoor courts and a partially covered outdoor stadium, an indoor arena, and eight indoor courts. The total complex will seat more than 7,600 people during major events. The plaza surrounding the tennis courts with its jasmine-covered court fences, covered walks, trellises, kiosks, and seating areas is programmed to host events throughout the year.

A geometric paving system of silver and black granite overlaid with a grid of palms and canopy trees unites the entire development. A pedestrian bridge connects the 360 Mall to the new retail space and hotel, while also serving as a gallery for fine art, media displays, and events.

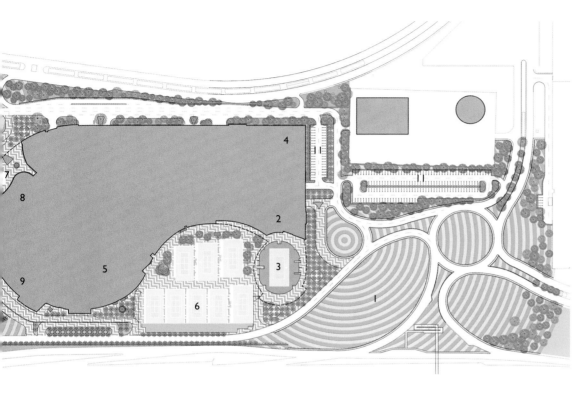

PLAN OF NEW COMPLEX WITH EXISTING RETAIL CENTER

1	Arrival Garden
2	Tennis Club
3	Indoor Tennis Stadium
4	Indoor Tennis Courts
5	Indoor Arena
6	Outdoor Courts Plaza
7	Cliff Gardens
8	Shopping
9	Hotel
10	Gallery Bridge
11	New Parking
12	Existing Parking
13	Existing Shopping Center
14	Existing Pools
15	Existing Mosque

Winter
Mounded arrival garden with
deciduous lawn and stone bands

Summer

top left: Palm allée from parking

top right: Glazed shopping mall

bottom left: Café garden with rain fountain

bottom right: Tropical arrival garden

Inside the retail, flanking each end of the corridors, two conservatories serve as major gathering spaces and the focus of restaurant venues. The main retail corridors and conservatories are covered by a glass roof that encourages the growth of gardens and more than 400 linear meters of green walls on the retail storefronts.

A water feature provides the focal point of the West Conservatory—a rain fountain randomly programmed with hundreds of water jets simulating the pattern of rain drops. Defining the rain fountain is a garden surrounded by large blocks of gold granite that double as casual seating spaces.

The Cliff Gardens mark the retail entrance at the ground level. A large glass curtain wall connects the exterior landscape to six restaurants defined by stone and plant-covered walls. Mirrored balls suspended from the ceiling visually connect the Cliff Gardens space to the West Conservatory above. Each of the three interior landscaped spaces incorporates a gold rough-hewn stone block that recalls the facades of the 360 Mall and the new tennis complex.

229

top: Courtside plaza

middle: Arrival plaza at mall and hotel

bottom: Arbor at tennis tournament court

William P. Clements Jr. University Hospital

Dallas, Texas

*above: Automobile entry
overlooking cypress grove*

This new state-of-the-art hospital provides 1.3 million square feet and 460 patient rooms at the University of Texas Southwestern Medical Center. The primary goal is to create a high-value landscape that contributes to the health and recovery of its patients. Sixty percent of the site is dedicated to open green space with plants carefully selected for their low water needs. A 15-acre grid of bald cypress trees planted along the hospital frontage in a meadow of buffalo grass will emphasize axial views to the hospital and serve as a wayfinding function to key hospital entries, activity centers, and patient areas. Seventy percent of the patient rooms will offer views of the meadow and roof gardens

designed in artful geometric patterns of stones, boulders, glass, and mirrors.

An additional two acres of outdoor space are dedicated to activity areas that include a garden for patients and a dining terrace for patients, hospital staff, and visitors. Under a canopy of bald cypress, the secured Patient Garden will provide extensive seating areas, planting gardens, walking paths, and therapy areas. The Dining Terrace will perform as an outdoor extension of both the Dining Pavilion and the adjacent cafeteria.

In addition to the outdoor activity areas, more than 3,000 feet of walking/jogging paths have been designed for the site,

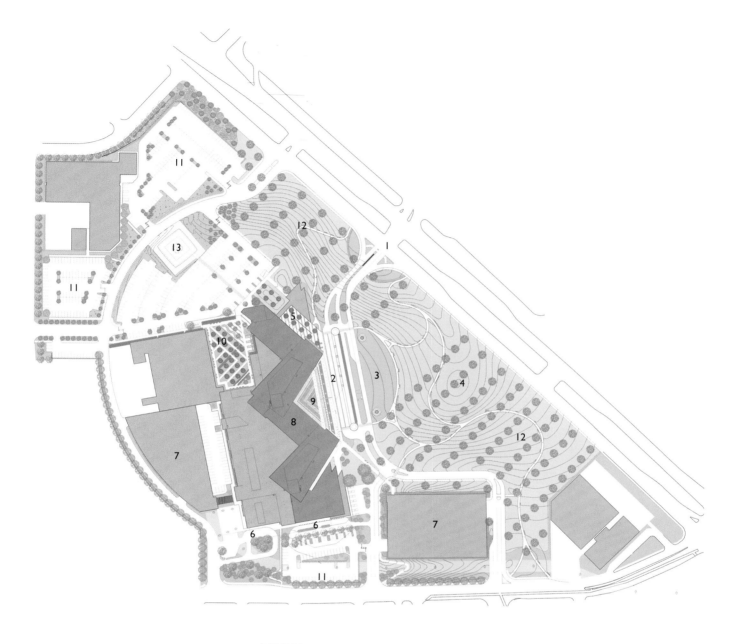

LANDSCAPE PLAN OF NEW CAMPUS

1	Entry	7	Parking Garage
2	Arrival Plaza	8	Hospital Tower
3	Fountain Green	9	Roof Garden
4	Rolling Meadow with Cypress Grove	10	Patient Garden
5	Dining Terrace and Pavilion	11	Parking
6	Emergency	12	Pedestrian Path
		13	Helipad

top and middle:
The Patient Garden

bottom: Ground-level
Dining Terrace

encouraging use by hospital workers, visitors, and patients as part of their health and recovery plans. A parking strategy includes two conveniently located parking structures for visitors and for staff. Only ten percent of the site is used for surface parking.

Two 16-foot-tall clear acrylic cylinders have been designed as sculptural fountains to frame the main hospital entrance and views from nearby Harry Hines Boulevard. With their cascading water the fountains will provide a calming effect as they change through the course of the day from a dark to a light turquoise color that gently reflects the sunlight, then transitions to a soft glow at night.

above: Hospital campus with cypress grove and fountains

Jewel Changi Airport

Singapore

above: Café overlooking garden and waterfall

Jewel at the Singapore Changi Airport is envisaged as a destination that will enhance Changi's air-hub status as it provides visitors with a multisensory experience of nature within a climate-controlled glass dome. A 5.4-acre park over interior retail space integrates unexpected features to attract adventurers of all ages. Gardens terrace down five levels to a central gathering space with informal amphitheater seating. At the center of the building visitors experience what is expected to be the world's tallest indoor waterfall, the 40-meter-high Rain Vortex, which will transform into a light-and-sound show in the evening.

Two trails begin at the Forest Valley floor and climb four stories to the Canopy Park, where a large pond is the source of a meandering waterfall that flows down the planted terraces. Trees grow on each of the terraced levels as if they were on a sloped mountain valley, their trunks growing tall and thin as they reach for the light transmitted through the giant glass roof above. Four Gateway Gardens—dramatic vertical-garden faces of the building—entice airport visitors to enter and experience the unexpected landscapes within.

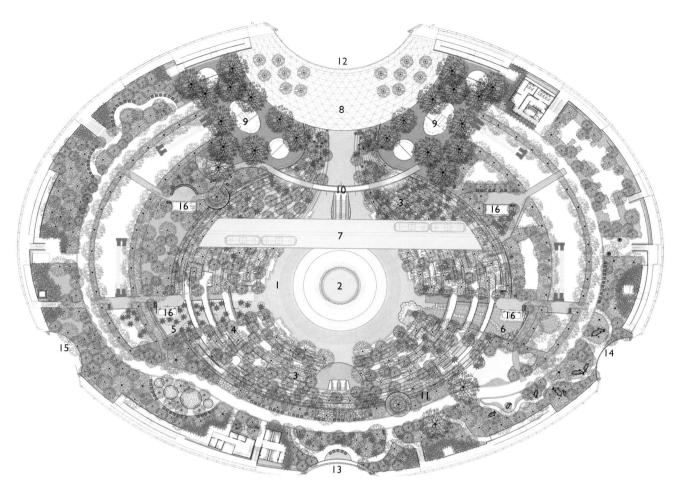

235

PLAN OF GARDEN

1 Forest Valley
2 Rain Vortex Pool
3 Forest Valley Terraced Planting
4 Valley Trail and Overlook Terraces
5 Palm Canyon
6 Bamboo Canyon
7 Airport Train

8   Event Plaza
9   Cafés
10 Flying Bridge
11 Overlook
12 North Gateway Garden (Below)
13 South Gateway Garden (Below)
14 East Gateway Garden
15 West Gateway Garden
16 Elevator

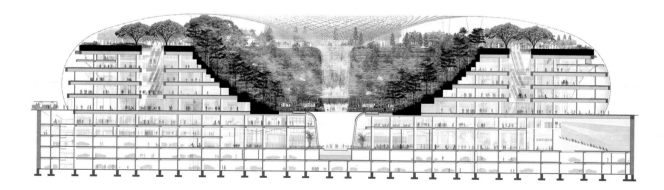

SECTION OF TROPICAL GARDEN

Natural materials, including wood, stone, water, mist, and more than 100 plant species, create the experience of a tropical forest valley. The climate within the building is of the utmost importance. Air movement and humidity are key factors in supporting the plants, as are the temperature and sunlight requirements. Generally people enjoy a cooler and drier indoor environment than do most truly tropical plants. In the Jewel the plant palette and the climate design have been carefully honed so that a designed landscape can thrive while visitors remain comfortable.

In addition to the garden walks and the light-and-sound show, there will be activities at the Canopy Park to attract visitors of all ages as well as food and beverage outlets where visitors will be able to enjoy al-fresco-like dining while admiring views of the Forest Valley.

Water cascade

Expedia Headquarters

Seattle, Washington

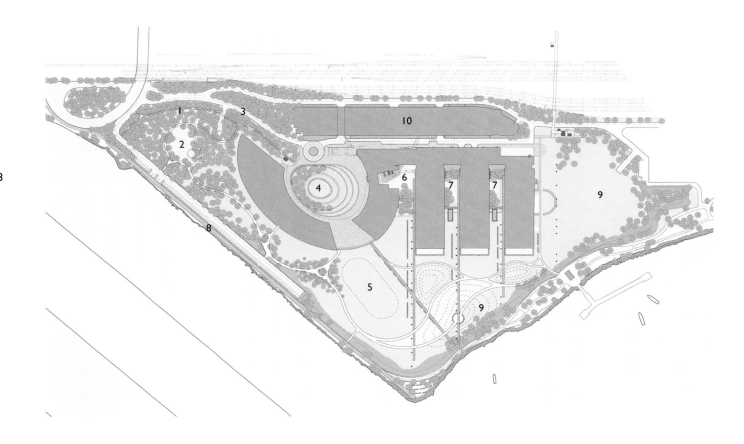

EAST-WEST SECTION AT ATRIUM

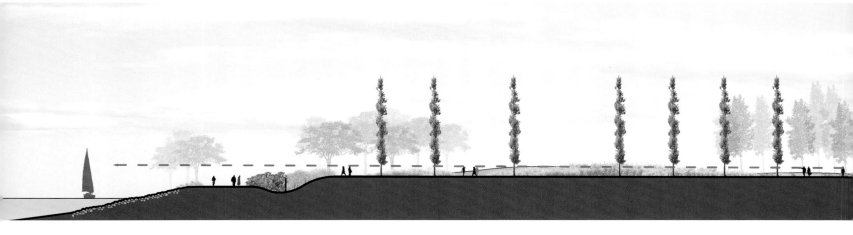

PUGET SOUND   HAHA WALL   CAMPUS GREEN

LANDSCAPE PLAN OF CAMPUS

Expedia's new headquarters sits on a generous 40.3-acre waterfront site with southern and western views across Puget Sound and beyond to Mount Rainier. The campus buildings, designed by architects Bohlin Cywinski Jackson with interiors by STUDIOS Architecture, include the Ellipse, which inscribes the Ring Courtyard, and the Finger buildings, which extend toward the waterfront and frame a series of interior landscape spaces, the Nexus and two atria.

On the land side the campus edge is defined by the Woods, a newly planted forest—composed of trees native to the Pacific Northwest—which creates an entry threshold for visitors and provides an essential buffer against the adjacent industrial rail yard. The Entry Drive leads visitors to a cobbled Arrival Court, which opens to the Ring Courtyard.

The Ring Courtyard is composed of a series of elliptical lawn terraces with a central disappearing fountain that can be quickly drained to provide a plaza space for gatherings and events. A grove of deciduous trees and crescent landforms create a counterpoint to the building entry and frame views out through a building aperture to the Campus Green and the waterfront beyond. The Campus Green, which is bordered by a series of gently mounded meadows of native grasses, is large enough to accommodate a number of recreational venues ranging from soccer, volleyball, and cricket to picnicking, sunbathing, and large and small meetings.

Between the Finger buildings lie outdoor courtyards—with irregular rows of columnar trees and linear bio-retention elements planted with iris—that gesture

239

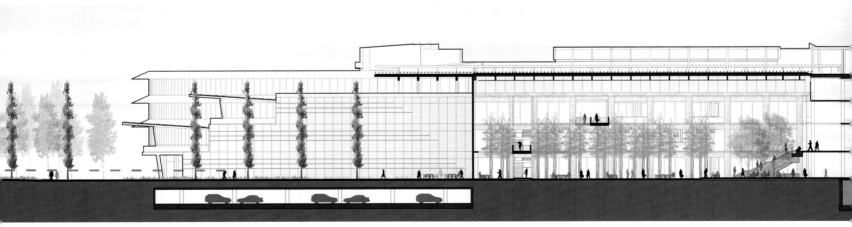

PARKING   ATRIUM

above: Campus Green

outward to the views. Behind the open courtyards, the planted atria can accommodate café seating, small and large meetings, and such presentations as music, art, and craft shows.

A series of linear stone paths extends out from the Finger buildings; they are crossed by curvilinear parklike paths that go into the Woods, which contains a quiet rhododendron-lined glade for special meetings.

The campus interior is separated from the public bike and jogging trails that run along the waterside public right-of-way by a linear ha-ha—a fence hidden in planting—which allows outward views while protecting the privacy of the interior campus. At the western perimeter of the site, the Promenade runs along Smith Cove, paralleling the public bike path and providing opportunities for fishing, launching small boats, and landing harbor ferries.

top left: Woodland entry drive

top right: Rhododendron glade

bottom: Foreshore promenade

Ring Courtyard at Arrival Court

COMPETITIONS
ONE FOR IKE AND TWO FOR DAN

Peter Walker

European tradition requires that all major public buildings and civic spaces be selected through a competition process. This custom has been going on for more than a century. Although with less consistency, many of the most distinguished public institutions in the United States have used the same method to select the concept and the designer for important monuments, memorials, and public spaces. For PWP competitions are an important part of an idea-directed practice, and we try to select ones that excite and challenge the office—that is, those competitions that require or allow the pursuit of a concept or idea. They are almost always for important sites and draw wide public interest, both by their purpose and formal beauty.

For better and worse, there generally is no engaged client to react during the design process. On the one hand, this offers a freedom to explore and interpret the design opportunities in ways not found in many typical projects. On the other hand, it

Dwight D. Eisenhower Memorial

Washington, D.C.

left to right: Stone and brick paving, paving detail, prairie-grass bands, flowering ground cover

poses the problem of lack of direction, an important part of any design. Curtailing client interaction limits the depth of information available, and, of course, there is little opportunity to engage the subjective interests of the client or jury. Some competitions eliminate even the final presentation, although it is more common these days to have an interim presentation generally dominated by professionals not directly connected to the client. Such interim presentations allow for questions and answers even if the jury is seldom present.

Since these limitations put emphasis on the information contained in or gleaned from the designer's prospectus, site visits, and independent research, the strength of the submission depends on the designer's conclusions and the ideas brought to the table. The explanation may not register with or please the jury—or finally the client—but

the effort is exhilarating. These efforts are intense, and whether one wins or loses, the final solutions provide useful experience.

Our office regularly submits to these competitions. Win or lose, they enable us to expand our imaginations and test our conceptual ideas. Here are three of our recent efforts—two losers and one winner. Along with the competition for the National September 11 Memorial, which is included in the project descriptions, they have been important to the practice over the last decade:
- Dwight D. Eisenhower Memorial, Washington, D.C. (2009);
- Jefferson National Expansion Memorial, St. Louis, Missouri (2010);
- Constitution Gardens, Washington, D.C. (2011).

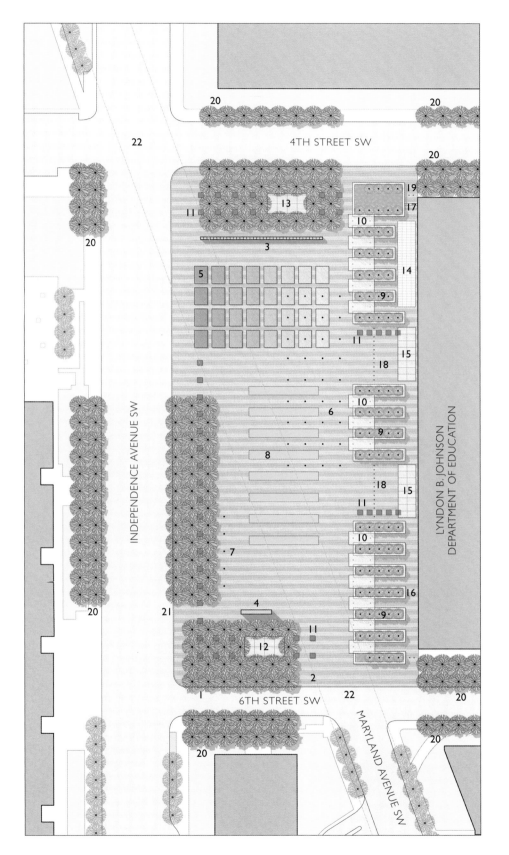

MEMORIAL PLAN 247

1   Colonnade of Trees
2   Kansas Brick and
    Gray Stone Pavement
3   The Wall of War
4   The Presidential Stele
5   The Normandy Fountain
6   Flags of Institutions
    (United States, United Nations,
    European Union, NATO, SEATO)
7   Flags of Allies
8   Prairie Grasses
9   Raised Stone Planters with
    Columnar Trees
10 Glass Canopies
11 Lantern Benches
12 Glass-enclosed Book Store
13 Glass-enclosed Ranger Station
    and Restrooms
14 Proposed Flush Skylight
    above Library
15 Glass Canopy
16 Service Lane
17 Stone Steps
18 Fixed Bollards
19 Movable Bollards
20 Additional Proposed Trees
21 Stone Curb
22 Historic Cartway

Prairie-grass bands on plaza

Grilled cast-bronze light benches

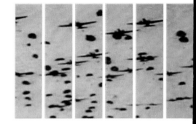

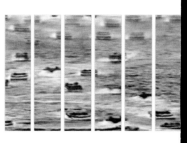

Dwight D. Eisenhower, like Washington, Lincoln, and Roosevelt, was elevated to stupendous heights by momentous times, a great general who became a strong president striving for world peace. Nevertheless, his story and accomplishments are passing from common knowledge. We therefore felt his memorial should have a strong educational component.

Our proposal for the Eisenhower Memorial began with a great urban square in Washington, D.C., planted with native prairie grasses and paved with golden Kansas bricks that symbolize Eisenhower's childhood roots and gray granite bands that recall the gray of West Point. The proposed square would be surrounded with formal bosques that reach across the surrounding street forming a graceful transition to the Lyndon B. Johnson Department of Education building. The bosques would be planted in a series of grids that suggest military precision.

We divided the open center of the square into two areas that symbolically depict war and peace and demonstrate the ways that Americans experienced Eisenhower's greatness: During the war they saw General Eisenhower in newsreels at the movies, and as postwar citizens they watched the Eisenhower presidency on the new medium of television.

For the War period, a long horizontal cast-glass segmented wall with a digitally enabled interior would show projected newsreels from World War II. These newsreels would emphasize the industrial scale of the war, the D-Day flotilla, aerial bombing, and tank warfare across a wide battlefield. A Normandy Fountain, dedicated to D-Day, would have standing water rectangles. When viewed through their sides, the rectangles would reveal the treacherous floor at Omaha Beach. The still water at the fountain's surface would reflect changes in the wind and weather, so important to Eisenhower's lonely decision to invade. Alongside, a regimented field of flags would represent the Allied Nations.

right: Open axial view toward the dome of the Capitol Building

below: Glass wall panels with internal images of World War II industrial-scale warfare as seen in Movietone newsreels

249

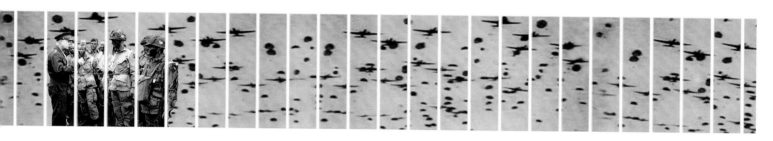

Bombing raids

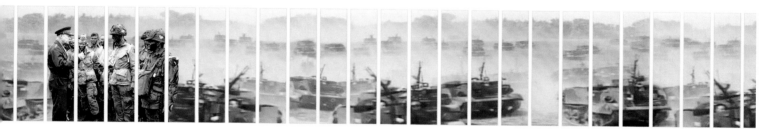

Tank battles

D-Day invasion

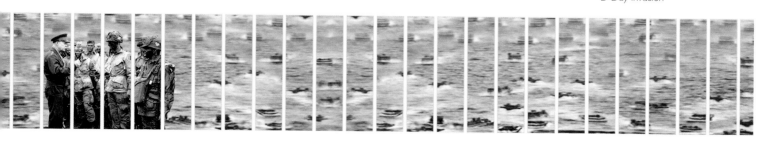

Landing on Omaha Beach

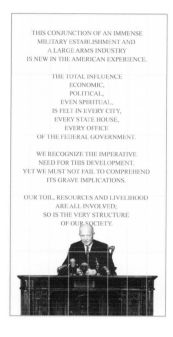

THIS CONJUNCTION OF AN IMMENSE
MILITARY ESTABLISHMENT AND
A LARGE ARMS INDUSTRY
IS NEW IN THE AMERICAN EXPERIENCE.

THE TOTAL INFLUENCE
ECONOMIC,
POLITICAL,
EVEN SPIRITUAL,
IS FELT IN EVERY CITY,
EVERY STATE HOUSE,
EVERY OFFICE
OF THE FEDERAL GOVERNMENT.

WE RECOGNIZE THE IMPERATIVE
NEED FOR THIS DEVELOPMENT.
YET WE MUST NOT FAIL TO COMPREHEND
ITS GRAVE IMPLICATIONS.

OUR TOIL, RESOURCES AND LIVELIHOOD
ARE ALL INVOLVED;
SO IS THE VERY STRUCTURE
OF OUR SOCIETY.

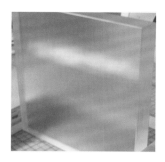

above: Glass stele with interior moving projection of Eisenhower speaking in the visual style of 1950s television

facing page top: View of presidential stele with flags of international organizations sponsored by President Eisenhower

bottom: View toward the Capitol with Wall of War and flags of World War II allies

For the Peace period, a digitally animated 70-foot cast-glass stele would feature a monumental 25-foot image of Eisenhower seated at his desk in the Oval Office while a list of his programs and speeches scrolls upward behind him. Here the images would suggest the style of early television broadcasts. Another field of flags would represent NATO nations. Within the grove behind the stele would lie a glazed bookshop and interpretive center. Beneath the groves of trees a series of internally lit cast-bronze benches would cast a soft golden glow across the square, while allowing the Wall of War, the Normandy Fountain, and the Presidential Stele to provide the major lighting of the memorial. The memorial would honor Eisenhower's life and provide an additional park for the city.

Unfortunately our proposal for the Eisenhower Memorial was not the winner.

Jefferson National Expansion Memorial

St. Louis, Missouri

top right: Allées planted with Kiley's proposed tulip poplars

top left: View of Arch toward the downtown with rebuilt museum and interpretive center below

bottom: Proposed museum interiors

Both the St. Louis Gateway and Constitution Gardens are previous failures, failures that were the product of both the client and the designer, who in both cases was Daniel Urban Kiley.

In 2010, after several unsuccessful attempts, the Gateway Foundation (a citizen fundraising organization) and the National Park Service (NPS) conducted a competition for the redesign of the park at the St. Louis Arch, including a new museum and interpretive center as well as a new 91-acre park on the East St. Louis side of the river.

The original memorial was the result of a competition held in 1947 and won by a team led by landscape architect Dan Kiley and architect Eero Saarinen. Both the glorious stainless steel Arch and the public garden at its base suffered many difficulties, but while the Arch was brilliantly realized, the garden failed at almost every level—ecologically and mechanically—with the result that it separates the Arch from the city, the Gateway Mall, the river, and, indeed, the whole region. Professional rivalries, financial limitations, unsolved site-specific conditions, and arbitrary field decisions by the client all contributed to a tragic failure of opportunity for all concerned.

Here are some of the factors contributing to the first failure:

- The designer's inability to remove or conceal the railroad tracks paralleling the river in front of the Arch meant that they remained in two large ugly ditches running the length of the site; these make the river's edge too steep for pedestrian use and cut off views of the river from

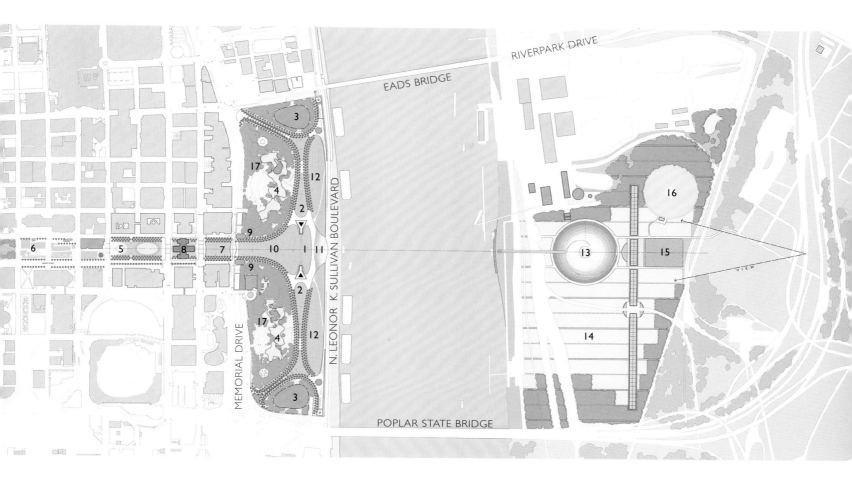

all parts of the site except at the great central stair and the Saarinen lookouts.

- The client accepted large amounts of imported earth-fill not called for in the design; this formed ten-foot mounds that separate the park from the downtown and the adjacent roadways, isolating the grounds from the normal life of the city.

- The design of the aging underground interpretive center was inadequate, and the existing entry to the museum and Arch does not meet current ADA requirements.

- Rosehill ash trees were substituted for the tulip trees specified by Kiley at the request of the local nurseryman, who had a large supply of ash trees; these trees never achieved the intended grand scale and are now dying off.

- Drainage, irrigation, lighting, and paving systems were cheaply installed in order to save money; they have subsequently collapsed.

- Ponds in the central lawns were "modified" from the Kiley design by client-requested changes in grading development and planting; the ill-formed ponds have subsequently suffered ecological collapse.

- A crude exposed-aggregate concrete grand stair was later installed; it did not follow Saarinen's formal design concepts or material, which are shown in the two sweeping concrete side stairs.

- Poor grading on the west side of the park destroyed the visual connection to the Gateway Mall and the old courthouse; a later parking garage and freeway interchange separate the park from the city to the north and south.

PLAN OF EXTENDED MEMORIAL

1 The Gateway Arch
2 The Allées
3 Future Institutions
4 Ponds
5 Kiener Plaza
6 City Garden
7 Luther Ely Smith Square
8 Old Courthouse
9 Elevator Pavilions
10 Skylights to Interpretive Center
11 Saarinen Stair
12 Bluff
13 Viewing Mound
14 The Center for Agricultural Well-being
15 Farmers Market
16 Gateway Geyser
17 Prairie Forest

254

top: Perspective from East St. Louis
with monumental viewing mound
and agricultural museum

bottom: Grounds of agricultural
museum and existing silos at the
river's edge

We were told about and shown these
installation errors by the NPS. There
seemed to be agreement that the
changes had materially contributed to
the park's failure. Our first steps were
to understand Saarinen's and Kiley's
intent. We read the complete file—gra-
ciously provided to us by the NPS—
which included many drawings and
sketches and a great deal of explanatory
correspondence and articles in which
historians discussed the differences between Kiley and the NPS leadership. The
correspondence included the demand
that Saarinen fire Kiley (his best friend)
and his sad, apologetic letter to Kiley. I
believe that if money could have been
found and the original designers had
been left in charge through the completion of the construction, the St. Louis

Arch Park would have been Dan Kiley's greatest work and perhaps the most important modern design achievement of the NPS of that era.

Our feeling at this point in the competition was that a respectful renewal of the park, correcting the client's previous errors of judgment and bringing the park up to modern ecological requirements, would be the wise and respectful direction to follow. After all, the changes collectively had caused the failure of the park. In large part, the original Kiley design made sense, practically and aesthetically. The required changes to the underground buildings and the allées were endorsed by the client, and there was an agreed-upon interest in the repair as well as sufficient funds to provide all of the remedies.

However, in 1996 a set of historic rules of interpretation had been established within the NPS. These rules required the NPS to attribute historic significance to the errors that had been established in the original park. This seemed preposterous on the face of it because this requirement would not allow the agreed-upon mistakes to be rectified. We did not believe that these directives would control the renewal of the park. It turned out that we were mistaken. Our design grew naturally out of the requirements for repair. The City's ambition to reconnect the downtown and mall could easily be remedied with regrading and the removal of the existing mounds. The City's request for added activity could be accommodated by regrading and planting the greens and revising and raising the "surreal ponds."

top: Reflecting pools with Kiley's proposed landscape of informal prairie and woodland

bottom: Nighttime NPS lectures in the prairie forest

256

above: Repaired bluff that allows assembly areas with river views

The site's northern and southern borders could be opened up to the natural grade of the riverfront entertainment areas and provide sites for such future public buildings as museums and public institutes. The riverbanks could be flattened to encourage congregation and celebration. The railroad tracks could be put underground and the raised banks lowered, thus restoring the river views. The riverfront could be enlivened by providing moorage for floating restaurants and other public venues. The cheap exposed-aggregate stairs could be reconstructed in the Saarinen manner. In short, changes could be made that would substantially realize the designers' original intentions. On the eastern shore, we proposed a monu-

mental grassed hill of sufficient size to compose with the scale of the Arch, the grassed riverbank, and rebuilt allées. Behind the hill, we proposed an outdoor agricultural museum and experiment station, open to the public.

We were told that we lost the competition for our violation of the NPS historic evaluation guidelines. At the jury, juror Laurie Olin asked us if we were willing to battle the NPS historians for years. We replied that we hoped it was time for the historic evaluation guidelines to be modified. Again, we were proven wrong.

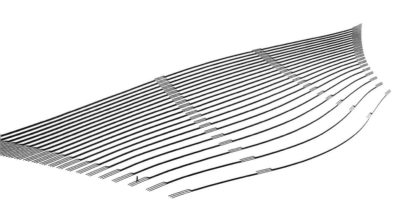

top: Nighttime celebration viewed
from bluff at river's edge

bottom: Proposed redesign of
Saarinen's grand staircase joining
the Arch to the river's edge

Constitution Gardens

Washington, D.C.

above: Proposed ice-skating rink and restaurant terrace

We are, however, able to close this essay with a win for Kiley.

The situation at Constitution Gardens was in many ways similar to the failure at the Jefferson National Expansion Memorial. The garden was built in 1976 for the Bicentennial celebration. It was designed by Kiley and the architect Charles Bassett of Skidmore, Owings & Merrill. As was the case in St. Louis, it had been built in haste and by 2011 was a total ecological disaster. The poor sub- and topsoil was collapsing, repeatedly drowning the trees and shrubs.

The pavements had cracked with the collapse of the soil, and the drainage systems had failed. Potable city water was used for irrigation and for the pond, which filled with site runoff, fouling the water and requiring repeated draining as well as cleaning away algae buildup. The precious and expensive water was used only once and then dumped into the Tidal Basin. We felt that a complete renovation was required, including a re-building of the sub- and topsoil and the drainage system. We foresaw a regrading of the entire site that would require tree moving, a new recycling water

259

*Section showing water purification
and recycling strategy*

SECTION THROUGH THE SEASONS

The complex beauty of seasonal change possible
with careful rebuilding of soil and drainage as well
as replacement of failing trees and understory

SUMMER

PLAN OF PROPOSAL

1	The Lake
2	Reflecting Basin – Model Boating and Winter Skating
3	Restaurant Pavilion
4	Meeting Plaza
5	Amphitheater
6	Flower Display
7	West Knoll
8	Vietnam Memorial
9	Birthday Meadow
10	Picnic Meadow
11	Sun-Bathing Lawn
12	Lock Keepers House
13	Viewing Lawn
14	56 Signers Memorial
15	World War II Memorial
16	Aeration Ring
17	Magnolia Island
18	Aeration Pool
19	Lincoln Memorial
20	National Mall

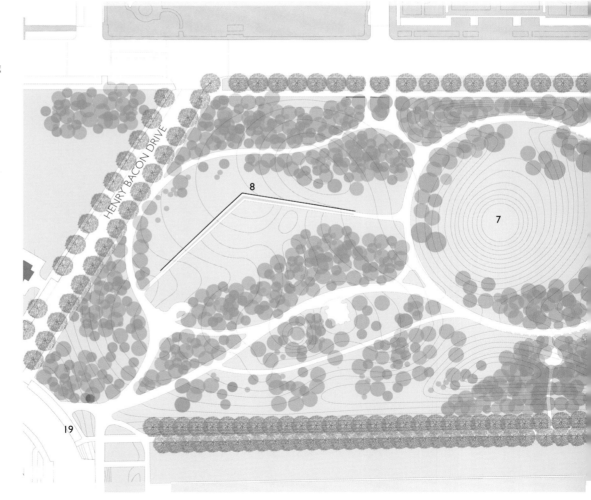

Section showing re-grading to block noise from passing cars and views of cars from pond-side path

View from Constitution Avenue

SPRING

The beauty of seasonal change is possible with careful rebuilding of soil and drainage along with replacement of failing trees and understory

top: Topographic revisions for removal of degraded soil

middle: Understory planting to recycle and purify irrigation water

bottom: Reforestation after soil and drainage are rebuilt

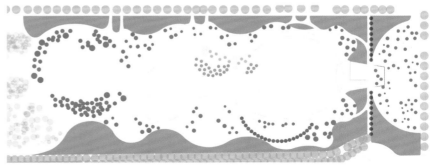

FALL   WINTER

CONSTITUTION AVENUE

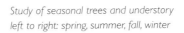

Study of seasonal trees and understory
left to right: spring, summer, fall, winter

Garden entry beside the relocated
Lock Keeper's House

*Proposed cobble-paved path
at water's edge with historic lighting
and benches*

*View of pond-side path, grass
amphitheater, and flower displays*

system to conserve water use, and a total refurbishing of all site construction, including lights, furniture, and pavements. There was need for new established-use areas and a new pavilion/restaurant/interpretive/public-service building. (The originally proposed building had never been realized.)

Many of the needed physical and ecological systems may not have been known by the designers or the NPS in 1975-1976. However, we were aware that the same NPS rules about historic interpretation that had been applied in St. Louis would likewise be applied to this competition. We therefore built a team that included the architect Rob Rogers, AIA, and Patricia O'Donnell, a distinguished landscape architect and history consultant who had been working on the restoration of the adjacent National Mall sponsored by the Trust for the National Mall.

Then, in 2012 we carefully crafted our major rebuilding proposal to repair the ecological damage within the NPS historic guidelines using NPS lights, benches, and so forth. Included in the ecological transformation were a series of new or improved recreational activity areas, such as provisions for winter ice skating, an informal amphitheater, an expansion area for celebrations related to both the Vietnam and World War II memorials, which had been built after the garden. Also included were more generous and graceful connections to the two new memorials. Facilities for fishing, skating, and model-boating were provided in the beautiful new pavilion designed by Rob Rogers, including several venues for formal and informal dining, a small book store and interpretive center, and a refurbished Lock Keeper's House, which would be moved into the garden.

This time we were successful.

facing page: Sunset view across the pond to restaurant, Washington Monument, and Capitol dome

264   ACKNOWLEDGEMENTS

PWP Landscape Architecture would like to express special thanks 265 to those whose work has made this book possible: Monica Way, Chris Walker, David Walker, Adam Greenspan, Maik Schaufuss, Su-Jung Park, Michael Dellis, Chris Dimond, Conard Lindgren, Pietro Bonomi, Steve Tycz, Eric Lees, Heath House, Mi Yang, Chelsea DeWitt, Conny Roppel, Marta Gual-Ricart, Janet Beagle, Amelia Starr, Sandy Harris (all from our staff), Mary Fawcett, and Anne Elizabeth Powell.

Special thanks go to Sarah Vance, our long-time friend and colleague, whose graphic design and visual talent enrich this book, as they have so often enriched our publications in the past.

Partners

PETER WALKER, FASLA, SENIOR DESIGN PARTNER

Education
Harvard University Graduate School of Design:
Master of Landscape Architecture, Jacob Weidenman Prize
for Outstanding Design Ability, 1957
University of Illinois: Graduate study in landscape
architecture, 1956
University of California, Berkeley: Bachelor of
Science in Landscape Architecture, 1955

Selected Teaching
Chairman, Department of Landscape Architecture,
University of California, Berkeley, 1997-1999
Charles Eliot Chair, Harvard University
Graduate School of Design, 1992
Adjunct Professor, Harvard University
Graduate School of Design, 1976-1991
Chairman, Department of Landscape Architecture
Harvard University Graduate School of Design, 1978-1981
Acting Director, Urban Design Program
Harvard University Graduate School of Design, 1977-1978
Visiting Critic, Massachusetts Institute of Technology, 1959
Instructor, Department of Landscape Architecture
Harvard University Graduate School of Design, 1958-1959

Selected Authorship
*Invisible Gardens: The Search for Modernism in the American
Landscape* with Melanie Simo. Cambridge: The MIT Press, 1994

Selected Awards
J.C. Nichols Prize for Visionaries in Urban Development,
Urban Land Institute, 2012
American Society of Landscape Architects Firm Award, 2012
Honorary Doctorate of Fine Arts, University of Illinois, 2008
Cooper-Hewitt National Design Award, 2007
Geoffrey Jellicoe Gold Medal, International Federation
of Landscape Architects, 2005
ASLA Medal, American Society of Landscape Architects, 2004
Thomas Jefferson Medal, University of Virginia, 2004
Centennial Medal, Harvard University, 2003
John R. Bracken Medal, Pennsylvania State University, 2003
Honorary Doctorate of Landscape Architecture,
University of Pretoria, South Africa, 2003
Institute Honor, American Institute of Architects, 1992
Resident, American Academy in Rome, 1991

DOUGLAS FINDLAY, FASLA, MANAGING PARTNER

Education
Harvard University Graduate School of Design:
Master of Landscape Architecture with Distinction,
Charles Eliot Traveling Fellowship, 1984
California Polytechnic State University, Pomona:
Bachelor of Science in Landscape Architecture, 1980

Professional Experience
PWP Landscape Architecture
Douglas Ross Findlay Landscape Architect
Michael Van Valkenburgh Associates
The SWA Group

JULIE CANTER

Education

> University of Pennsylvania School of Design:
> Master of Landscape Architecture, 2006
> Cornell University: Bachelor of Science in Landscape
> Architecture, 2003

Professional Experience

> PWP Landscape Architecture
> Thomas Balsley Associates
> Environmental Design & Research

MICHAEL DELLIS

Education

> Cornell University: Bachelor of Science in
> Landscape Architecture with Honors, 2003

Professional Experience

> PWP Landscape Architecture
> FTB Urban Design

F. CHRISTOPHER DIMOND, FASLA

Education

> University of Georgia: Bachelor of Landscape Architecture, 1977

Professional Service

> Chair, Landscape Architecture CEO Roundtable
> President, Vice President, Board, Board Emeritus,
> Landscape Architecture Foundation
> ASLA National Executive Committee and Board of Trustees

Professional Experience

> PWP Landscape Architecture
> HNTB Corporation

ADAM GREENSPAN

Education

> University of Pennsylvania School of Design:
> Master of Landscape Architecture, 2001
> Wesleyan University: Bachelor of Arts in Studio Art
> and Sociology with Honors, 1994

Professional Service

> Board, Landscape Architecture Foundation

Professional Experience

> PWP Landscape Architecture
> Hargreaves Associates

SANDRA FRANZOIA HARRIS

Education
    University of California, Santa Barbara: Bachelor of
    Arts in Business Economics, 1981

Professional Experience
    PWP Landscape Architecture
    Hughes Aircraft Company

CONARD LINDGREN

Education
    California Polytechnic State University, San Luis Obispo:
    Bachelor of Science in Landscape Architecture, 1991

Professional Experience
    PWP Landscape Architecture
    Sasaki Associates
    The SWA Group

TODD MEAD

Education
    University of Colorado, Denver: Master of
    Landscape Architecture, 1991
    University of Wisconsin, Madison: Bachelor of Science in
    Natural Resources, 1981

Professional Service
    ULI Hines Competition Jury
    ULI Advisory Panel, Houston, Texas
    ULI Advisory Panel, Port Elizabeth, South Africa

Professional Experience
    PWP Landscape Architecture
    Civitas
    Design Workshop

MARTIN POIRIER, FASLA

Education
    Harvard University Graduate School of Design:
    Master of Landscape Architecture, Jacob Weidenman Prize
    for Outstanding Design Ability, 1986
    Michigan State University: Bachelor of Landscape Architecture, 1976

Professional Service
    Harvard University Graduate School of Design, Alumni Council
    Ambassadorship Co-Chair
    San Diego Downtown Partnership, Urban Design Advisory Board
    City of San Diego Community Forest Advisory Board,
    Founding Member

Professional Experience
    PWP Landscape Architecture
    Spurlock Poirier Landscape Architects
    The Spurlock Office
    The Office of Peter Walker Martha Schwartz
    Kurt Meyer Partners
    POD, Inc.
    Johnson, Johnson and Roy
    Smith, Hinchman & Grylls

JAY SWAINTEK

Education

State University of New York College of Environmental
Science & Forestry: Master of Landscape Architecture, 1996
Pennsylavnia State University: Bachelor of Science
in Economics, 1991

Professional Experience

PWP Landscape Architecture
Vita Planning & Landscape Architecture
Suzman & Cole Design Associates
Royston Hanamoto Alley & Abey
Copley Wolff Design Group

DAVID WALKER, FASLA

Education

Harvard University Graduate School of Design:
Master of Landscape Architecture with Distinction, 1992
Rhode Island School of Design: Bachelor of Fine Arts
in Landscape Architecture with Honors, 1983

Professional Experience

PWP Landscape Architecture
POD, Inc.
William D. Warner, Architects & Planners
Searle & Searle Landscape Architects and Planners

Current Employees

Past Employees

SENIOR ASSOCIATES
Carmen Arroyo
Steve Tycz

ASSOCIATES
Janet Beagle
Eustacia Brossart
Chelsea DeWitt
Brian Gillett
Heath House
Laurel Hunter
Justin Jackson
Kazu Kobayashi
Su-Jung Park
Conny Roppel
Chris Walker
Monica Way
Mi Yang

STAFF
William Benge
Pietro Bonomi
April Deerr
Annette Flores
Jane Gillette
Marta Gual-Ricart
Darryl Jones
Maria Landoni
Eric Lees
Seth Rodewald-Bates
Maik Schaufuss
Amelia Starr
Anna Thompson
Jamie Yousten

Steven Abrahams
Branden Adams
Wolfgang Aichele
Costis Alexakis
Verda Alexandra
Pablo Alfaro
Duncan Alford
Annie Amundsen
Kira Applehans
Jeanne Aquilino
Michael Averitt
Sierra Bainbridge
C. Timothy Baird
Ka-t Bakhu
Patricia Bales
Alec Balliet
Arthur Bartenstein
Daniel Baur
John Bela
Katherine Bennett
Jim Bensman
Eva Bernhard
Lisa Beyer
Clair Bobrow
Kari Boeskov
Michelle Bond
Theodore Booth
Charles Brandau
Kimberly Brigati
Annegret Brinkschulte
Jennifer Brooke,
   Associate
Michael Brooks,
   Partner
Carl Brown
Clint Brown
Hugo Bruley
Paul Buchanan,
   Associate
Neil Budzinski
Marni Burns
Caroline Burzan
Cameron Campbell
Katherine Cannella
Alexis M. Canter

Scott Carman
Ave Carrillo
Dixi Carrillo
Juliana Carvalho Do Val
Elizabeth Chaffin
Alexandre Champagne
Conway Chang
Kay Cheng
Sara Chisum
Young Joon Choi
Shanai Chung
Ana Coello
Philippe Coignet
McKenna Cole
Steel Colony
David Condron
April Cottini
Jennifer Cox
Gina Crandell
James Curtis
Kitty Daniel
Kyle Davis
Andrew Day
Lisa Daye
Kimberlee De Jong
Cathy Deino Blake,
   Partner
Yasmin Del Rio
John Dennis
Lisa Derlplace
Jan Design
Albert DeSilver
Christine Dianni
James Dinh
Juliana Do Val
Danielle Dobeck
Matthew Donham,
   Partner
Nadine Dreyer
Kathryn Drinkhouse
Michelle Dubin
Mark Dugger
Alexander Dunkel
Katherine Eastman
Shadi Edarechi Gilani

Claire Eddleman
Daphne Edwards,
   Associate
Liz Einwiller,
   Partner
Sara Fairchild
Claire Fellman
Andrew Findlay
Nicole Findlay
Andreas Flache
Henry Fleischmann
Raeven Flores
Martha Folger
Joanna Fong
Anna Forrester
Ron Frank
Peter Frankel
Philip Frankl
Marta Fry
Yue Fu
Yoriko Fukushi
Thomas Gage
Charles Gamez
Lisa Ganucheau
Trudy Garber
Kimberly Garza
Alke Gerdes
Liette Gilbert
Shauna Gilles-Smith
Robert Gilmore
David Godshall
Marshall Gold
Elizabeth Gourley
Sarita Govani
Jeff Grandview
Jim Grimes,
   Associate
Megan Griscom
Zi Gu
Christopher Guillard
Anne Guillebeaux
Lauren Hackney
Leesa Hager
James Haig Streeter
Karolos Hanikian

Jane Hansen
Sarah Hanson
Claudia Harari
Tim Harvey
Jim Hellinger
Robert Hewitt
Chester Hill
Kelly Hitzing
Martin Hoffman
Martin Holland
Roxanne Holt
Jia J. Hu
Hermes Illana
Dorothée Imbert
Christine Jepson
Laura Jerrard
Bruce Jett
Bin Jiang
Dirk Johnson
Mark Johnson
William Johnson,
   Partner
Rachel Johnson
Collin Jones,
   Partner
David Jung
Raphael Justewicz
Ide Kakiko
Martin Kamph
Bill Kaszubski
Akshay Kaul
Ken Kawai
Tatsuya Kawashima
Ester Kerkmann
Rhonda Killian
Kari Koch
Ethan Kong
Brett Kordenbrock
Elizabeth Krason
Benjamin Kuchinsky
Matei Kucina
Sarah Kuehl,
   Partner
David Kunugi
Denise Kupperman

Sonja Kurhanewicz
Grace Kwak
Bruce Lall
Shelby LaMotte
Patrick Lando
Nicolas Lantz
Tom Leader,
  Partner
Daria Lebedeva
Heeyoung Lee
Ihsien Lee
Paul Lee
Steven Lee
Terence Lee
Mark Lehmann
Mia Lehrer,
  Partner
Margaret Leighly
Randy Lein
Christian Lemon
Christopher Leong
Carol Lesh
Mandy Leung
Frannie Levaggi
Leah Levy
Noah Levy
Jaruvan Li
Qindong Liang
John Lichter
Phoebe Lickwar,
  Associate
Lynda Lim
Feng Lin
Hanyu Liu
Jennifer Livingston
Tarlton Long
James Lord,
  Associate
Gilat Lovinger
Leor Lovinger
Henry Lu
David Madison
Elliot Maltby
Mark Maniaci
Rita Manna

Jennifer Marano
Esther Margulies
Robin Massingill
Anuradha Mathur
Mary Pat Mattson
Anne McDonald
Greg McGuire
Hope McManus
Paula Meijerink
Gabriel Meil
Alex Mena
David Meyer,
  Partner
Danielle Meyer
Wes Michaels
Kirsten Miller
Leo Miller
Wendy Miller
Nicole Miner
Javier Miranda
Yasuhiko Mitani
Toru Mitani
Jacob Mitchell
Moritz Moellers
Tim Mollette-Parks
Kjersti Monson
Cary Moon
Duane Moore
Julie Morris
Christian Mueller
Timothy Muhlebach
Shuichi Murakami
Mary Muszynski
Wemerson Nader
Kevin Napoli
Serena Nelson
Susan Nettlebeck
Diane Nickelsberg
Thomas Nideroest
Makoto Noborisaka
Joseph Nootbaar
Michael Odum
Hans Oerlemans
Michael Oser
Peter Osler

Sebine Otten
Mignon O'Young
Sally Pagliai
Pamela Palmer
Nikos Papadopoulos
Jose Parral
Grace Pasol
John Pearson
Joaquin Pedrin
Nathan Pepple,
  Associate
Jacob Petersen
Johanna Phelps
Laura Phipps
Meaghan Pierce-Delaney
Susan Pinto,
  Associate
A.J. Pires
Marie Rafalko
Scott Rahder
Gustavo Ramirez
Lawrence Reed
Sandra Reed,
  Senior Associate
Elizabeth Reifeiss
Ellen Reihsaus
Martin Rein-Cano
Kerry Ricketts
Peter Rier
Dee Rizor
Isabel Robertson
Robert Rock
Maura Rockcastle
Denise Rogers
Jay Rohrer
Robert Rombold
Melody Rose
Lisa Roth
Gabriel Rustini
Matthew Safly
Martha Sanchez
Michael Sanchez
Sen Sanjukta
Jennifer Sasson,
  Partner

Christopher Scavone
Doris Schenk,
  Associate
Alex Schuknecht
Kim Schumacher
Martha Schwartz
Keith Scott
Nina Seelos
Joon Seo Park
Monica Servé
Christopher Sherwin
Donald Shillingburg
Jason Shinoda
Taya Shoup,
  Associate
Heidi Siegmund
Paul Sieron,
  Partner
Ramsey Silberberg
Rafael Silberblatt
Lucia E. Silva
Carina Simmchen
Melanie Simo
Tony Sinkosky,
  Partner
Jeffrey Smith
Ken Smith
William Smith
Carol Souza
Angelika Spies
Kelly Spokus,
  Associate
Gisela Steber,
  Associate
Rachel Stevens
Meghan Storm
Chella Strong
Kimberly Stryker
Margaret Stueve
Bryan Suchy
Lital Szmuk
Kendra Taylor
Jane Tesner
Emma Thomas
Eric Thomasson
Gina Thornton

John Threadgill
Randy Thueme
John Tornes
Maria Toscano
Jennifer Toy
Katharina Trinks
James Trulove,
  Partner
Christian Tschumi
Lisa Tsui
Jeffrey Ulm,
  Associate
Ludwig Vaca
Sarah Vance,
  Partner
Christopher Varesi
Nadine Waldmann
Peter M. Walker Jr.
Michael Wasser
Matthias Wehrle
Christian Werthmann,
  Associate
Nicholas Wessel
Jamie White
Timothy Wight
Jane Williamson,
  Partner
Stella Wirk
Aichele Wolfgang
Lauren Wong
Molly Wood
Robert Wood
Kathryn Woods
Mei Wu
Eddy Wylie
Roderick Wyllie
James Yan
Ah-Ram Yang
Chris Yates
Anna Lisa Ybarra
Jeena Yi
Wan-chih Yin
Wan Yin
Shuochen Zheng
Michael Zonta

Consultant Teams

PROJECTS

Barangaroo Reserve, Sydney, Australia

Client: Barangaroo Delivery Authority
    Craig van der Laan, CEO; John Tabart, former CEO
    Bob Nation, David McCracken, Tony Gulliver, Joseph Paonesa,
    Peter Funder, Phil Paris, Daryl Kite, Brian ten Brinke, David Young
Barangaroo Board of Directors 2015: Terence Moran, Chairman
Barangaroo Design Excellence Review Panel (2009-2012):
    Paul Keating, Chairman; Chris Johnson, Angelo Candalepas,
    Bridget Smyth, Oi Choong, James Weirick, Leo Schofield
Lead Designer: PWP Landscape Architecture
Landscape Architect of Record with Lend Lease for
    Landscape Construction: Johnson Pilton Walker
Architect: WMK for Baulderstone (John Andreas, Cecelia Wells)
Accessibility Consultant: Morris Goding
Arborist and Horticulturalist: Norcue (Stuart Pittendrigh)
Chief Stone Mason and Quarry Operations Manager: Troy Stratti
Civil and Structural Engineers: Robert Bird Group, Aurecon
Construction Manager: Evans and Peck
General Contractors: Baulderstone, Lend Lease
    (Barry Murphy, Kieron Little)
Geotechnical Engineer: Douglas Partners
Graphics, Signage, and Wayfinding Designer: Emery Studio
Historic Interpretation Consultant: Judith Rintoul
History and Arts Consultant: Peter Emmett
Hydraulic Engineer: Warren Smith and Partners
Landscape Construction Observation Manager:
    Tract Landscape Architects (George Gallagher, Matthew Easton)
Landscape Contractor: Regal Innovations
Lighting Engineer: Webb Australia Group
Marine Engineer: Hyder Consulting (Peter Masters)
Plant Procurement Nursery: Andreasens Green
Soil Scientist: SESL (Simon Leake)
Transportation Engineer: Halcrow

Cleveland Clinic, Cleveland, Ohio

Client: Cleveland Clinic Foundation
Landscape Architect of Record: Epstein Design Partners
Architect: NBBJ (Columbus)
Accessibility Consultant: Margen + Associates
Arborists: Fred J. Robinson & Associates,
    Dr. Robert E. Moon & Associates
Civil Engineer: Michael Benza & Associates
Fountain Designer: Dan Euser Waterarchitecture
Illustrator: Christopher Grubbs
Irrigation Designer: ISC Group
Paving Consultants: Mark Smallridge & Associates,
    ACRI Stone & Tile Consulting
Transportation Engineer: CDM Smith

Colorado Esplanade, Santa Monica, California

Client: The City of Santa Monica
Local Landscape Architect:
    Artecho Architecture + Landscape Architecture
Arborist: Michael T. Mahoney
Civil and Structural Engineer: Fuscoe Engineering
Electrical Engineer: IDS Group
Graphics, Signage, and Wayfinding Designer: Ph.D, A Design Office
Irrigation Designer: ISC Group
Lighting Designer: Atelier Ten
Paving Consultant: Mark Smallridge & Associates
Transportation Engineer: Fehr and Peers
Urban Designer: Cityworks

"Finite Infinite", Beijing, China

Client: Beijing Garden Expo
Consulting Landscape Architect: BAM (Jacob Schwartz Walker)

Glenstone, Potomac, Maryland

Client: The Glenstone Foundation
Phase One
Architect: Gwathmey Siegel and Kaufmann Associates Architects
Arborist: Bartlett Tree Experts
Field Ecologist and Meadow Consultant: Jeff Wolinski
Horticulturalist: Michael Jackson
Irrigation Designer: Sweeney and Associates
Master Stone Mason: Travis Callahan
Wetland and Pond Consultant: Angler Environment
Phase Two
Architect: Thomas Phifer and Partners
Agricultural and Soil Management Consultant: Matthew Rales
Arborist: Bartlett Tree Experts (Tim Zastrow)
Civil Engineer: VIKA (Maryland)
Environmental Engineer: BuroHappold Engineering
Fountain Designer: Dan Euser Waterarchitecture
Fountain Engineer: Biohabitats
General Contractor: HITT Contracting
Graphics, Signage, and Wayfinding Designer: 2 x 4
Horticulturalist: Darrel Morrison
Irrigation Designer: Sweeney and Associates
Lighting Designer: ARUP (New York)
Master Stone Mason: Phillip Dolphin
Meadow Consultant: Larry Weaner Landscape Associates
Owner's Representative: Mark G. Anderson Consultants
Soil Scientist: Pine & Swallow Environmental
Structural Engineer: Skidmore, Owings & Merrill (Dmitri Jajich)

Marina Bay Sands Integrated Resort, Singapore

Client: Las Vegas Sands
Architect: Safdie Architects
Local Landscape Architect and Horticulturalist: Peridian Asia
Art and Water Feature Consultants: Ned Kahn, Howard Fields
Civil, Structural, and Transportation Engineer:
    ARUP (Australia, Hong Kong, and Singapore)
Graphics, Signage, and Wayfinding Designer: Pentagram
Lighting Designer: Project Lighting Design
Palm Consultant: Donald Hodell from University of California Extension

Nasher Sculpture Center, Dallas, Texas

Client: The Nasher Foundation
Architect: Renzo Piano Building Workshop
Associate Architect: The Beck Group
Agronomist, Soil Scientist, and Irrigation Designer: Jeffrey L. Bruce &
    Company (Jeffrey Bruce, Charles Dixon, Richard Yates)
Arborist and Horticulturalist: Dr. Robert E. Moon & Associates
Civil Engineer: Halff Associates
Fountain Designer: Dan Euser Waterarchitecture
Graphics, Signage, and Wayfinding Designer: 2 x 4
Lighting Designer: Horton Lees Brogden Lighting Design
Paving Consultant: Mark Smallridge & Associates
Tree Procurement and Relocation Consultant: Environmental Design

National September 11 Memorial, New York, New York

Client: The National September 11 Memorial & Museum Foundation
Architect: Michael Arad
Architect of Record and Associate Architect: Davis Brody Bond
Pavilion Architect: Snøhetta
Arborist: Paul Cowie & Associates
Civil Engineer: Parsons Brinkerhoff
Concrete and Structural Soil Contractor: Navillus
Electrical Contractor: Five Star Electric
Fountain Designer: Dan Euser Waterarchitecture
Geotechnical Engineer: Mueser Rutledge
Irrigation Designer: Northern Designs (Mike Astram)
Lighting Designer: Fisher Marantz Stone
Mechanical/Electrical/Plumbing Engineer: Jaros, Baum & Bolles
Paving Consultant: Mark Smallridge & Associates
Plumbing Contractor: 4 J's
Site Metal Supplier: Skyline
Soil Scientist: C.R. Dixon & Associates
Stone Supplier: Port Morris Tile & Marble
Structural Engineer: WSP Cantor Seinuk
Sustainability Consultant: Viridian Energy & Environmental
Tree Care Consultant: Bartlett Tree Experts
Tree Installation Consultant: Kelco Landscaping
Tree Relocation Consultant: Environmental Design
Vector Control (rodents): Global Environmental Options
    (Stephen Frantz)

Newport Beach Civic Center and Park, Newport Beach, California

Client: The City of Newport Beach
Architect: Bohlin Cywinski Jackson
Arborist: Michael Mahoney
Bunny Maker: Cemrock
Cactus and Succulents Consultants: Gary Lyons, Kevin Coniff
Civil, Structural, and Sustainability Engineer: ARUP (San Francisco)
Graphics, Signage, and Wayfinding Designer: Ph.D, A Design Office
Illustrator: Chris Grubbs
Irrigation Designer: ISC Group (Ray Arthur)
Lighting Designer: ARUP (San Francisco)
Meadow Consultant: John Greenlee
Native Plants Consultant: Tree of Life Nursery (Mike Evans)
Palm Consultant: Donald Hodel from University of California Extension
Paving Consultant: Mark Smallridge & Associates
Soil Scientist: Pine & Swallow Environmental

Samsung Seocho, Seoul, South Korea

Landscape Architect of Record: Samsung Everland
Architect: KPF
Architect of Record: Samoo Architects

Sydney Olympic Park, Sydney, Australia

Client: Sydney Olympic Park Authority
    (formerly Olympic Coordination Authority)
Landscape Architects: HASSELL (Tony McCormick),
    PWP Landscape Architecture, Bruce Mackenzie Design
Civil Engineer: Kinhill Engineers
Cost Estimator: Northcroft QS Partnership
Environmental Education and Interpretation Consultant:
    Natural & Cultural Heritage (Christine O'Brien)
Environmental Management: Fathom Consulting
Forest and Natural Heritage Conservation Consultant:
    Old Cassowary Consulting
Geotechnical and Landfill Engineer: RH Amaral and Associates
Illustrators: Christopher Grubbs, Barry Mitchell
Irrigation and Water Management: Fluid Flow
Lighting, Solar, and Communications Designer: Barry Webb and
    Associates
Park Management Planner: Jeff Floyd
Recreation Planner: HM Leisure Planning
Soil Scientist: SESL (Simon Leake)
Water Management and Irrigation Designer: WET Consulting

University of Texas at Dallas, Dallas, Texas

Client: University of Texas at Dallas
Phase One
Accessibility Consultant: Accessology
Architectural Planning Consultant: David Neuman
Civil and Structural Engineer: Charles Gojer & Associates
Code Consultant: Schirmer Engineering
Cost Estimator: Davis Langdon Adamson
Electrical Engineer: Blum Consulting Engineers
Fountain Designer: Dan Euser Waterarchitecture
Horticulturalist: Dr. Robert E. Moon & Associates
Irrigation Designer: James Pole Irrigation Design
Lighting Designer: Horton Lees Brogden Lighting Design
Structural Engineer for Trellis: Werner Sobek
Transportation and Parking Engineer: Fehr and Peers
Phase Two
Local Landscape Architect for Construction Observation:
    MCV Landscape Architecture (Melanie Vanlandingham)
Accessibility Consultant: Assessology
Civil and Structural Engineer: Charles Gojer & Associates
Cost Estimator: Garza Program Management
Electrical and Mechanical Engineer: Yaggi Engineering
Fountain Designer: Aquatic Design & Engineering
Geotechnical Engineer: Terrecon
Horticulturalist: Dr. Robert E. Moon & Associates
Hydrologic Engineer: Sherwood Design Engineers
Irrigation Designer: James Pole Irrigation Design
Land Surveyor: Steven J. Lafranchi & Associates
Paving Consultant: Mark Smallridge & Associates

IN PROGRESS

China Resources, Shenzhen Bay, China

Client: China Resources Company Limited
Architects: KPF, Goettsch Partners, RTKL (Los Angeles)

Expedia Headquarters, Seattle, Washington

Client: Expedia, Inc.
Architect: Bohlin Cywinski Jackson
Interior Architect: STUDIOS Architecture
Civil and Structural Engineer: KPF
Development Manager: Seneca Group
Entitlements Consultant: Bassetti Architects
Geotechnical Consultant: Hart Crowser
Mechanical/Electrical/Plumbing Engineer:
    Affiliated Engineers and WSP
Parking Consultant: Graelic
Security Consultant: Aronson Security Group
Waterfront Consultant: Reid Middleton

Jewel Changi Airport, Singapore

Client: Changi Airport Group, CapitaLand Mall Asia
Local Landscape Architect and Horticultural Consultant:
    ICN Design International
Architect: Safdie Architects
Architect of Record: RSP Architects Planners & Engineers (Singapore)
Acoustic Engineer: ARUP (New York)
Art and Natural Phenomena Designer: The Exploratorium
Climate Control, Environmental, and Mechanical/Electrical/Plumbing
    Engineer: Atelier Ten
Façade, Glazing, and Structural Engineer: BuroHappold Engineering
Fountain Designer: WET Design
Lighting Designer: Lighting Planners Associates
Local Structural Engineer: RSP Architects Planners & Engineers (Singapore)
Mechanical/Electrical/Plumbing Documenter: Mott MacDonald
Soil Scientist: Kevin Handreck

Khiran Pearl City Marina, Khiran, Kuwait

Client: Tamdeen Group
Local Landscape Architect: Cracknell
Architect: RTKL (London)
Hotel Architect: RTKL (London)
Local Architect of Record and Civil, Mechanical/Electrical/Plumbing, and
    Structural Engineer: SSH Design
Fountain and Pool Designer: Aquatic Design & Engineering
Lighting Designer: Scott Lighting
Parking Consultant: Walker Parking Consultants
Plant Acquisition Consultant: Greenfields Agriculture

Kuwait International Tennis Complex, Kuwait City, Kuwait

Client: Tamdeen Group
Local Landscape Architect: Cracknell
Architect: RTKL (Dallas)
Hotel Architect: RTKL (London)
Architect of Record: PACE
Arena Designer: Sports Concepts
Civil, Mechanical/Electrical/Plumbing, and Structural Engineer: PACE
Fountain Designer: Aquatic Design & Engineering
Lighting Designer: T. Kondos Associates
Local Approvals Consultant: OHA Engineering Consultant
Parking Consultant: Walker Parking Consultants
Plant Acquisition Consultant: Greenfields Agriculture
Tennis Design Consultant: Artyrees (Richard Reese)

Transbay Transit Center and Mission Square, San Francisco, California

Client: Transbay Joint Powers Authority
Architect: Pelli Clarke Pelli Architects
Architect of Record: Adamson Associates Architects
   (Los Angeles, Toronto)
Accessibility Consultant: McGuire Associates
Accessibilty for the Blind Consultant: Chris Downey Architect
Acoustic, Voice/Data/Telecom, and Security Consultants:
   Shen Milsom & Wilke (San Francisco, Chicago), WSP (San Francisco)
Arborists: Barrie Coate and Associates, Stephen Batchelder Consulting
Artists: James Carpenter, Julie Chang, Tim Hawkinson,
   Jenny Holzer, Ned Kahn
Civil Engineer: ARUP (San Francisco)
Civil, Geotechnical and Transportation Engineer, Rail Facilities,
   Highway/Bridge, Tunnel Ventilation, Extreme Event and Risk,
   Pedestrian Circulation Operations Analysis, and
   Fire/Life Safety Consultant: ARUP (San Francisco)
Cost Estimator: Davis Langdon (San Francisco)
Design Structural Engineer: Schlaich Bergermann & Partner
Emergency Communication and Mass Notification Systems Consultant:
   Rolph Jensen & Associates
Façade Access (Window Washing) Consultant: Lerch Bates & Associates
Façade Consultant: Vidaris
Fountain and Mechanical/Electrical/Plumbing Engineer:
   Fountain Source Engineering and Design
Graphics, Signage, and Wayfinding Designer:
   WRNS Studio (San Francisco)
Horticulturalist and Palm Consultants: The Palm Broker (Jason Dewees),
   Donald Hodell from University of California Extension, Golden Gate
   Palms & Exotics (Gary Gragg)
Illustrator: Steelblue
Irrigation Designer: ISC Group
Landscape Lighting Designer: Horton Lees Brogden Lighting Design
Lighting Designer: Auerbach Glasow French Architectural Lighting
   Design and Consulting

Mechanical Controls Consultant: HMA Consulting
Mechanical/Electrical/Plumbing Engineer: BuroHappold Engineering
Mechanical/Electrical/Plumbing Engineer of Record: WSP (San Francisco)
Plumbing Engineer: Mechanical Design Studio
Risk and Vulnerability Consultant: URS/AECOM, DVS Security Consulting
Soil Scientist: Pine & Swallow Environmental
Structural Engineer: Thorton Thomasetti (Los Angeles)
Sustainability Consultant: BVM Engineering
Sustainability Engineer: Atelier Ten
Vertical Transportation Consultant: Edgett Williams Consulting Group
Vibration Consultant: Wilson Ihrig & Associates
Waterproofing Consultant: Henshell & Buccellato
Wetland Consultant: Rana Creek Living Architecture
Wind Consultant: RWDI Consulting Engineers and Scientists

University of Texas at Austin, Austin, Texas

Client: University of Texas at Austin
Accessibility Consultant: Accessology
Civil, Mechanical/Electrical/Plumbing, and
   Structural Engineer: Jose I. Guerra
Code Consultant: Jensen Hughes
Cost Estimator: Garza Program Management
General Contractor: Flintco
Horticulturalist: Dr. Robert E. Moon & Associates
Irrigation Designer: James Pole Irrigation Design
Paving Consultant: Mark Smallridge & Associates

William P. Clements Jr. University Hospital, Dallas, Texas

Client: University of Texas Southwestern Medical Center
Architect: RTKL (Dallas)
Accessibility Consultant: Accessology
Building Envelope Consultant: WJE Associates
Building Security Consultant: RTKL (Dallas)
Civil Engineer: JQ Infrastructure
Cost Estimator: Construction Cost Systems
Electrical Engineer: Smith Seckman Reid
Fire Protection/Code Reviewer: AON Fire Protection Engineering
Fountain Consultant: Dan Euser Waterarchitecture
Fountain Designer: Aquatic Design and Engineering
Geotechnical Engineer: Terracon Consultants
Graphics, Signage, and Wayfinding Designer: Chandler Signs
Horticulturalist: Dr. Robert E. Moon & Associates
Irrigation Designer: James Pole Irrigation Design
Lighting Designer: The Lighting Practice
Paving Consultant: Mark Smallridge & Associates
Structural Engineer: Walter P. Moore
Transportation Engineer: Kimley-Horn and Associates
Utility Relocation Consultant: Halff Associates
Wind Consultant: CPP Wind Engineering & Air Quality Consultants

COMPETITIONS

Dwight D. Eisenhower Memorial Competition
Lead Designer and Project Manager: PWP Landscape Architecture
Architect: James Carpenter Design Associates
Graphics, Signage, and Wayfinding Designer: 2 × 4
Lighting Designer: Fisher Marantz Stone
Local Designer and Project Director:
    Oehme, Van Sweden and Associates

Jefferson National Expansion Memorial Competition
Landscape Architect: PWP Landscape Architecture
Urban Designer: Civitas (Mark Johnson)
Architect: Foster + Partners (David Nelson, Spencer DeGray)
Local Architect of Record: Mackey Mitchell
Accessibility, Code, Fire, and Safety Consultant: Code Consultants
Agronomist: C.R. Dixon & Associates
Art Integration Consultant: Ned Kahn Studios
Civil Engineer: Cole & Associates
Community Outreach Consultant: Vector Communications
Cost Estimator: Davis Langdon
Cultural Landscape Historian: Dorothée Imbert
Economic Development Consultant: HRA
Graphics, Signage, and Wayfinding Designer: 2 × 4
Historic Setting and Section 106 Consultant: Quinn Evans Architects
Hydraulic Engineer: M3
Illustrator: Christopher Grubbs
Lighting Designer: George Sexton Associates
Local Transportation Engineer: CBB
Mechanical/Electrical/Plumbing, Structural, and Sustainability Engineer:
    BuroHappold Engineering
Mobility Transit Consultant: MIC
Program and Visitation Consultant: Lord Cultural Resources
Tree Relocation Consultant: Environmental Design
Western Expansion Historian: James Ronda

Constitution Gardens Competition
Landscape Architect: PWP Landscape Architecture
Architect: Rogers Marvel Architects
Historic Landscape Architect: Heritage Landscapes (Patricia O'Donnell)
Acoustic Engineer: Jaffe Holden
Arborist: Paul Cowie & Associates
Architectural Historic Preservation Consultant: EHT Traceries
Ecologist: Great Ecology
Environmental Engineer: BuroHappold Engineering
Graphics, Signage, and Wayfinding Designer: C&G
Horticulturalist and Public Landscape Maintenance Consultant:
    F2 Environmental Design
Interpretive and Interactive Graphic Designer: Local Products
Lighting Designer: Fisher Marantz Stone
Open Space Programmer: Biederman Redevelopment Ventures
Soil Scientist: Pine & Swallow Environmental

Awards

2015

AIA Pennsylvania Chapter Citation Award
Newport Beach Civic Center and Park,
    Newport Beach, California
Client: City of Newport Beach
Architect: Bohlin Cywinski Jackson

American Society of Civil Engineers Orange
    County Chapter – Sustainable Engineering
    Project of the Year Award
Newport Beach Civic Center and Park,
    Newport Beach, California
Client: City of Newport Beach
Architect: Bohlin Cywinski Jackson

Architizer A+ Awards – Jury Award
Barangaroo Reserve, Sydney, Australia
Client: Barangaroo Delivery Authority

Australian Institute of Landscape Architects –
    New South Wales President's Award
Barangaroo Reserve, Sydney, Australia
Client: Barangaroo Delivery Authority

Banksia Foundation Sustainability in Design,
    Build Award – Buildings, Landscapes and
    Infrastructure
Barangaroo Reserve, Sydney, Australia
Client: Barangaroo Delivery Authority

Infrastructure Partnerships Australia –
    Project of the Year
Barangaroo Reserve, Sydney, Australia
Client: Barangaroo Delivery Authority

World Architecture News – Waterfront Award
Barangaroo Reserve, Sydney, Australia
Client: Barangaroo Delivery Authority

2014

AIA Honor Award Orange County Chapter
Newport Beach Civic Center and Park,
    Newport Beach, California
Client: City of Newport Beach
Architect: Bohlin Cywinski Jackson

European Center at The Chicago Athenaeum
    Green Good Design Award
Newport Beach Civic Center and Park,
    Newport Beach, California
Client: City of Newport Beach
Architect: Bohlin Cywinski Jackson

2013

AIA Honor Award –
    Regional and Urban Design
National September 11 Memorial
    New York, New York
Client: National September 11 Memorial &
    Museum Foundation
Architect: Michael Arad
Associate Architect: Davis Brody Bond

American Public Works Association Southern
    California Chapter Project of the Year
Newport Beach Civic Center and Park,
    Newport Beach, California
Client: City of Newport Beach
Architect: Bohlin Cywinski Jackson

ASLA Honor Award – Design
Novartis Headquarters, Basel, Switzerland
Client: Novartis Pharma AG

Green Globe Awards –
    10 Year Sustainability Achievement Award
Sydney Olympic Park, Sydney, Australia
Client: Sydney Olympic Park Authority

2012

ASLA Firm Award to PWP Landscape
    Architecture: The highest award bestowed
    on a firm in recognition of distinguished
    work that influences the profession

ASLA Honor Award – Design
National September 11 Memorial,
    New York, New York
Client: National September 11 Memorial &
    Museum Foundation
Architect: Michael Arad
Associate Architect: Davis Brody Bond

Engineering News Record New York Award of
    Excellence – Hardscape / Landscape
National September 11 Memorial,
    New York, New York
Client: National September 11 Memorial &
    Museum Foundation
Architect: Michael Arad
Associate Architect: Davis Brody Bond

Retail & Leisure International (RLI) Global
    Award – International Shopping Center
Marina Bay Sands Integrated Resort, Singapore
Client: Las Vegas Sands
Architect: Safdie Architects

2011

Singapore Urban Redevelopment Authority
    President's Design Award –
    Design of the Year
Marina Bay Sands Integrated Resort, Singapore
Client: Las Vegas Sands
Architect: Safdie Architects

2010

AIA Excellence Award – Design
Transbay Transit Center, San Francisco,
    California
Client: Transbay Joint Powers Authority
Architect: Pelli Clarke Pelli Architects

Silicon Valley Business Journal –
    Green Project of the Year
Graduate School of Business Knight
    Management Center, Palo Alto, California
Client: Stanford University

2008

ASLA Landmark Award
Tanner Fountain, Cambridge, Massachusetts
Awarded to Peter Walker with
    The SWA Group
Client: Harvard University

2007

ASLA Honor Award – Design
UBS Tower (One North Wacker Drive),
    Chicago, Illinois
Client: John Buck Company
Architect: Goettsch Partners

Cooper-Hewitt National Design Award to
    PWP Landscape Architecture Annual award
    to honor lasting achievement in Ameri-
    can design for excellence, innovation, and
    exemplary work in urban, park, and garden
    design

2006

ASLA Award of Excellence – Communications
Land Forum, Berkeley, California

2005

ASLA Honor Award – Design
Stanford University Medical Center Campus,
    Parking Structure 4, Palo Alto, California
Client: Stanford University

2004

ASLA Honor Award – Design
Nasher Sculpture Center, Dallas, Texas
Client: The Nasher Foundation
Architect: Renzo Piano Building Workshop

ASLA Honor Award Northern California
    Chapter – Design and Planning
Jamison Square and Riverfront District Open
    Space Plan, Portland, Oregon
Client: Portland Parks and Recreation
Portland Development Commission

ASLA Merit Award – Design
Saitama Plaza, Saitama, Japan
Client: Saitama Prefectural Government

ASLA Merit Award – Design
The American Center for Wine, Food and Arts,
    Napa, California
Client: Copia
Architect: James Steward Polshek

Illinois Contractors Association Gold Award –
    Excellence in Landscape
UBS Tower (One North Wacker Drive),
    Chicago, Illinois
Client: John Buck Company
Architect: Goettsch Partners
Contractor: Walsh Landscape Construction

2003

ASLA Honor Award – Planning
Highbrook Business Park, Auckland,
    New Zealand
Client: Highbrook Development

2002

AIA Honor Award – Design
Sony European Headquarters, Berlin, Germany
Client: Sony Corporation
Architect: JAHN

AIA Pennsylvania Citation Award for Excellence
Pixar Animation Studios, Emeryville, California
Client: Pixar Animation Studios
Architect: Bohlin Cywinski Jackson

ASLA Merit Award Oregon Chapter – Design
Jamison Square, Portland, Oregon
Client: Portland Parks and Recreation,
Portland Development Commission

Chicago Magazine Best of Chicago –
    Best Streetscape
UBS Tower (One North Wacker Drive),
    Chicago, Illinois
Client: John Buck
Architect: Goettsch Partners

2001

Banksia Foundation Infrastructure
and Services Award – Water Reclamation and
    Management Scheme
Sydney Olympic Park, Sydney, Australia
Client: Sydney Olympic Park Authority

United Nations Environment Program –
Global 500 Role of Honor Award
Sydney Olympic Park, Sydney, Australia
Client: Sydney Olympic Park Authority

2000

ASLA President's Award of Excellence
Landmarks Series, Spacemaker Press
Publisher: Peter Walker
Associate Publisher: James Truelove

Australian RiverCare Water Management
    Award – Homebush Bay
Sydney Olympic Park, Sydney, Australia
Client: Sydney Olympic Park Authority

Australian Stormwater Industry
Association Award
Sydney Olympic Park, Sydney, Australia
Client: Sydney Olympic Park Authority

Banksia Foundation Gold Award
Sydney Olympic Park, Sydney, Australia
Client: Sydney Olympic Park Authority

Urban Land Institute International Award –
    Large Scale Mixed-Use
Sony European Headquarters, Berlin, Germany
Client: Sony Corporation
Architect: JAHN
Developer: Tishman Speyer

Credits

PHOTOGRAPHY

Tom Adams
28, 29, 30

Randy Anderson
96, 98, 99, 100

Barangaroo Delivery
Authority
60, 65, 67, 72, 78–79,
82–83, 86–87, 88–89,
foldout 67

Gerry Campbell
17, 18, 25, 20, 21, 24, 25,
39

Dixi Carillo
20, 24, 25, 35, 38

William Cho
198

Scott Frances
134

Getty Images / Pool
176–177

Tim Harvey
50

Jim Hedrich
13, 42, 43

Lower Manhattan
Development
Corporation
57, 147

David Meyer
33, 39

Hiko Mitani
46, 47

Atsushi Nakamichi
48

National Oceanic
and Atmospheric
Administration (NOAA)
146

Neoscape
234, 236, 237

Pamela Palmer
46, 52

Joseph Paonessa
72

PWP Office
16, 18, 19, 22, 23, 30, 31,
32, 33, 34, 36, 37, 44, 50,
51, 53, 56, 57, 58, 59, 67,
70, 72, 73, 80–81, 84–85,
86–87, 88–89, 90–91,
92–93, 94, 96, 98, 99,
102–103, 104–105, 115,
116, 118, 119, 132, 133,
135, 138–139, 140–141,
142, 143, 144, 145, 148,
152, 153, 154, 155, 156,
158, 159, 160, 161, 162–
163, 164–165, 166–167,
168–169, 170–171, 178,
180, 181, 182–183, 184,
185, 186, 187, 190, 191,
192–193, 196, 197, 200,
201, 202, 203, 214, 218,
219, 246, 249, 251, 252,
257, 266, 267, 268, 269,
foldouts 67, 137

Ethan Rohloff
118–119, 120–121

Troy Stratti
76–77

Hiroshi Tonaka
49

Transbay Joint Powers
Authority
205, foldout 207

Tim Wight
39, 53

Eiji Yonekura
44, 45

Sydney Olympic Park
Authority
106, 110, 111, 112, 113,
114, 117, 119

Alan Ward
11, 172–173, 174–175

Jacob Schwartz Walker
125, 126, 127, 128, 129,
130–131

World Trade Center
Memorial Foundation
146, 147, 149, 150, 152

ILLUSTRATIONS

Chris Grubbs
108, 109, 150, 151,
220–221, 240, 248, 249,
250, 254, 255, 256, 257

Lauren Hackney
137, 195, 258, 259, 261,
262, foldouts 136, 261

Chris Walker and
Pietro Bonomi
68, 69, 74, 75, 209, 210,
211, 212, 215, 217, 222,
224, 225, 227, 228, 229,
230, 232, 232, 240,
242–243, foldouts 66, 217